Letting Go of the Never-Agains
A Journey of Love and Loss

By

Jennifer Rae Trojan

COPYRIGHT NOTICES

© 2018 Jennifer Rae Trojan

All rights are reserved. Any unauthorized use, sharing, reproduction or distribution of these materials in any way by any means, electronic, mechanical or otherwise, is prohibited. No portion of these materials may be reproduced in any manner whatsoever without the express, written consent of the author.

Published under the Copyright Laws of the Library of Congress of the United States of America by:

Jennifer Rae Trojan Publishing
West Chicago, Illinois

International Standard Book Number
978-0-9978633-3-8

Cover Design
Kim Stephenson – PawPrintsPix
Photography

OTHER BOOKS

BY

JENNIFER RAE TROJAN

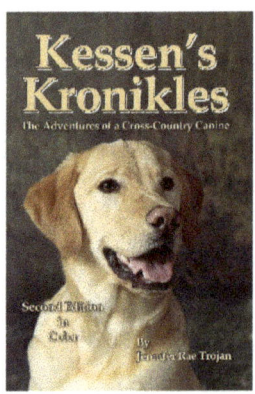

DEDICATION

To the man who filled

my life with joy…

…and whose passing

took it all away.

TABLE OF CONTENTS

INTRODUCTION 1
   When Tragedy Strikes 3

PRELUDE TO A FAIRY TALE 9
   A Sign of the Times 11

THE FAIRY TALE BEGINS 13
   Wishful thinking 15
   Time Gets in the Way 21
   When Sparks Fly 39
   The Courtship 42
   The Wedding 46

FROM THIS DAY FORWARD 55
   To Have 57
   To Hold 61
   For Better 64
   For Worse 71
   For Richer 75

For Poorer 88

In Sickness 95

In Health 98

To Love and To Cherish 103

Until Death Do Us Part 116

AFTER THE FAIRY TALE ENDS 131

The Journey Begins 133

Reality Sets In 142

Prince Charming Remembered 148

Grief Galore 154

Family Is Just A Concept 164

Crisis of Faith 173

Life Goes On 182

CONCLUSION 199

Holding the Winning Hand 201

The Author 219

Acknowledgements 221

INTRODUCTION

When Tragedy Strikes

To some individuals, this story might seem like an attempt to find a degree of closure to the unimaginable loss of a loved one. To others, my story might just be an effort to make sense of something that shouldn't have occurred but happened in spite of all indications to the contrary. Then again, it just might be the telling of a love story that began over sixty years ago and ended long before its time.

Believe me, it's not one of those stories that claims to never have said the words *I'm sorry* because throughout the years, those sincere words reverberated numerous times within our household. But, having the courage to say those words in the midst of a disagreement led to what solidified the commitment to our marriage. Perhaps we just took turns saying them but made sure they were said so that moving on was within our grasp. Parts of my story won't always be in chronological order, but it is the journey that mattered.

To be blunt…life is just a crapshoot. Doesn't matter all that much if one takes care of oneself, eats right, exercises and has annual checkups because the bottom line is that cancer just doesn't care. Sure, we play the odds and take care of ourselves, but in the end, cancer holds the aces in the deck of cards and determines the outcome.

To some, writing this story might seem self-serving on my part, and they would be totally correct. Because I needed to find reasons for what happened, I believed my story was meant to be told…not just for my sake but for those who find themselves in similar circumstances wondering how to make sense of all that happened.

I spent a lot of time thinking about the never-agains…those memories of events that popped into my mind at various times of the day. Because each one reminded me that I will never again do those things with my soulmate, I thought that perhaps I needed to find a way to let go of those never-agains or to at least lessen the awful sadness that accompanied the reminders of the love lost forever. Was I kidding myself by thinking such an endeavor was even possible or just trying to find a way to survive the horrible sadness that filled my days?

Nevertheless, I was determined to find a way to come to terms with my situation. I realized that this quest of mine might very well be either a short term or a life-long process for me; and if

I were successful in any time frame, would I be happy with the outcome? My mission was filled with a roller coaster of surprising emotions but was unquestionably a journey I needed to take.

If you are one of the unlucky ones who looks for comfort due to an unimaginable loss, I certainly hope you find some sort of relief from your sadness. On the other hand, if you are one of the lucky ones and still have your loved one beside you, be sure to treasure each moment of every day. Believe me…those moments and days are riches beyond belief and definitely not to be taken for granted…even if your loved one leaves socks on the floor, forgets to DVR your favorite television programs or doesn't notice the numerous items of laundered clothing hanging in the utility room that need to be put in closets. At the end of the day or at the end of their lives, these minor irritations are all such truly insignificant issues.

The bottom line…our loved ones leave us much too soon or leave us with words left unsaid because of the circumstances. Say what you need to say to your loved one while you can. The greatest gifts you give to him or to her are those last words of love and concern. Saying those words are the comforting gifts that last throughout all of the regrets that follow when tragedy occurs. Believe me…I speak from first-hand experience…

PRELUDE TO A FAIRY TALE

A Sign of the Times

It was the winter of 1953 when snow and ice filled the crowded streets of the city, and lawn chairs marked shoveled parking spots not to be ignored by those individuals who didn't bother to clear their own parking area. It was the unspoken law of the neighborhood not to take one of those shoveled spots. Surprisingly, most people respected that regulation lest they incur the wrath of their neighbor who labored tirelessly removing the snow from the space in front of his or her house. Some undeclared rules were not to be disregarded.

Parents talked to their children about walking miles and miles to and from school in the blustering snow, and no one had a choice of mealtime foods since the kitchen wasn't designated as a fast-food establishment. Safety wasn't a concern since doors were left unlocked, youngsters rode the subway trains by themselves, and no one thought twice about walking a few blocks through the neighborhood at night.

Those years of innocence have long past, but there are certain fond memories that rumbled around one's mind…memories that go unchanged and never forgotten due to their significance. One such memory floated around my mind and maintained a permanent place in my heart. It began like most fairy tales and might have maintained the status of a great fairy tale if not for the ending. I'll let you, the reader, decide for yourself as my story unfolds…

THE FAIRY TALE BEGINS

Wishful Thinking

Once upon a time in a northside neighborhood of Chicago on a street lit by the clouded light of an ancient street light, a group of young boys played hockey on the uneven surface of the ice-laden city street. The players were not shielded with padding from head to toe as professional hockey players were, nor did the boys even use a regulation hockey puck. Instead, they were kept warm with heavy coats, thick scarves, hand-woven knit hats and worn gloves. Discarded and very well-used, store-bought broom sticks were replacements for not having their own hockey sticks, and the puck might be a can of sardines pilfered from one of the player's pantries. Their lack of appropriate uniforms and equipment was not a concern…the game was still hockey. Nothing mattered except for the sound of the makeshift puck hitting the uneven ice, the sound of the broom stick connecting with the puck and the players jockeying for control of the sardine can. Game on!

As the boys played in spite of the freezing weather, most didn't know they were being observed from the second-floor window facing the makeshift ice rink. From the warmth of my living room, I closely watched the boys enjoying the camaraderie of a team sport in the midst of the bone-chilling weather. Personally, I thought their actions were a bit silly in terms of sliding around on the icy surface vying for a smack at a sardine can, but that thought was just my perspective. Being a girl who was not really interested in the value of the sport, I probably wasn't the best evaluator of their kind of fun.

I did, however, take note of their seriousness with regard to the game. Nothing mattered to them except the sound of the broom hitting the sardine can and its flying through the air toward a non-existent net. It didn't matter if someone called the triumph of a successful goal; it was the game that counted and the fun involved in playing.

I, on the other hand, watched as they circled, bumped and prodded each other in an attempt to gain control of the sardine can…the puck. I thought it was rather laughable that they weathered the icy winds for such a game with a broom and a sardine can. Little did I know that in the special group of boys gathered around that ancient street light was someone who would, in years to come, become my soulmate and the love of my life. My Prince Charming was in that circle of friends, and I didn't even know it at the time.

There was one boy in particular who glanced up at the second-floor window and tentatively brushed his knit hat with his hand as if he were waving to me. He did it in such a way that the other boys didn't see it as flirting…just adjusting his hat. I chose to believe the hat ruse was a definite wave of approval directed entirely toward me since I had the prime spot in the audience, and no one else was watching.

I continued to watch that young boy as he flew around the somewhat jagged ice hoping that he might look my way again. However, he continued to concentrate on the game and never looked up again that night. After all, he was a young boy among his friends, and no one his age bothered with girls…especially since I was someone's sister and totally out of bounds.

But, the feeling of that moment when our eyes met was something I had never experienced before. Sure, it was just a fleeting moment and perhaps he was really just adjusting his hat in the chilly weather. Nevertheless, I chose to believe that he was waving at me, and that tentative wave was something special shared by both of us.

If I only knew in my youth what knowledge I would gain in my adult life, the journey would have been much easier. However, would access to that information have limited the adventure or the excitement? It would all be so much easier, but would it be as much fun in the end? I think not…

Never again would I appreciate the innocence of that initial spark of youthful attraction as I watched that young boy zig-zag around the makeshift ice rink in the terrible, frigid weather. Experiencing that startling emotion as he touched his hat in a cautious wave to my second-floor bleacher seat was an unforgettable moment. Sardine cans would forever take on new meaning, brooms would always have a special connotation and that young boy, who glanced up at me with a bit of a wave, would someday find a permanent place in my heart. I had my first clue to the fairy tale and didn't even know it.

Time Gets in the Way

Several weeks passed and not once did I see that young boy and his teammates playing hockey in the chilly weather again that year. Perhaps the less than frigid weather made their ice rink no longer suitable for a game of hockey but became just an ordinary street filled with melting snow. Maybe, getting older changed their interests as they went their separate ways in school, in sports and in other adventures.

Some remained in the public school, while others including myself, transferred to the Catholic school. I won't say it was the nearby Catholic school because it wasn't. The jaunt to school in the morning, traveling back and forth at lunch time since the school didn't have a lunchroom and the journey back home at the end of the school day was no marathon, but it wasn't a quick trip either. Those city blocks are long, but since each day held new experiences, the daily trek didn't seem to matter.

Going to the Catholic school was quite a change from the public school. Not only was it my introduction to staunch religious beliefs governed by the nuns but was also the beginning of a great friendship with a latch-key kid.

I had heard rumors of those brave kids, but I never met one until going to the Catholic school. My latch-key friend actually had a key to her house and easy access without parental control. What an amazing concept!

Each morning, I'd walk two blocks to her house, and we'd take the journey to school together...rain or shine. Passing the candy store that was rumored to have a *creepy person* as an owner was always somewhat scary but also an exciting experience…at least for me. We mostly hoped that we wouldn't see him, but there was a small part of me that wondered what I would do if I caught a glimpse of the rumored *creepy person*. Let's face it…I never even knew what a *creepy person* might look like much less come in contact with one. After all, I was a sheltered Catholic school girl. Nevertheless, each school day held the apprehension of seeing that person as we quickly walked past the store. My latch-key friend never worried about it at all. I, on the other hand, worried about everything. You name it…I'd worry about it.

    Further down the block was the public school. Thursday was Spaghetti Day, and as we walked past the school building, the aroma of mouthwatering spaghetti sauce permeated the air. That aromatic experience made my spartan lunch waiting for me at home seem completely uninteresting.

Lunch was available for a quarter for Catholic school kids, but both my latch-key friend and I didn't have a quarter. Because our parents made sacrifices in order for us to attend the Catholic school, our asking for lunch money somehow seemed ungrateful. However, the aroma of that special spaghetti sauce was a bit overwhelming at times and played havoc with our digestive senses.

One day, my friend invited me to have lunch with her the following Friday. I really wanted to have that unsupervised lunch with my latch-key friend. Nevertheless, I needed to get permission from my mother. At first, Mom was a bit reluctant to leave two girls to their own devices and food choices, but she finally relented. Once her permission was given, I eagerly ventured into the world of my new friend…the latch-key world!

The occasion was totally exciting and had the air of such a grownup experience. Going into an apartment totally devoid of adults was unheard of in my sheltered world. I was beside myself with feelings of self-importance. How lucky was I, and what did I do to deserve such a friendship? The total experience was just overwhelming.

Since Fridays were designated as fish-only days for Catholics, I knew we were going to have some type of fish for lunch. While my friend prepared the meal, I spied the traditional sardine can that reminded me of that frigid winter night when the young hockey player gave a slight wave in my direction. Now, I had never seen or had sardines before, and my reminiscing ended quickly when my latch-key friend informed me that it was my lucky day…my sardine sandwich had the heads! The heads? Fortunately, she was just kidding and from then on, I knew we'd be good friends forever.

My Catholic school experience continued for years and encompassed the strict observance of rules as well as the ongoing reluctance to disobey the nuns at all costs…especially if parental notification were involved. The nuns had no tolerance for childish behaviors nor did our parents if disobedience were reported.

There was, however, one year in elementary school that stands out in my memory regarding the Catholic school experience and has direct relevance to my fairy tale. Entering the seventh grade meant moving to the second floor of the school building and having a new teacher. My latch-key friend and I were upper level now; and as far as we were concerned, we were headed towards graduation in the future.

The anticipation of meeting the new teacher was overwhelming. After all, this nun would ultimately prepare us for the eighth grade and eventual graduation. My latch-key friend and I were used to strict adherence to rules. Our former nuns had no patience for any silliness during the school day and no sign of a sense of humor.

Imagine our complete surprise when we were greeted by a nun who was the youngest nun we had ever seen. She had the sweetest face and was enthusiastically welcoming us to the seventh grade. Was this a trick? Was she an imposter? I was suspicious since I had never been greeted in such a friendly manner by a nun but was also strangely mesmerized by her most gentle demeanor. After welcoming us to the classroom and giving us our seating assignments, the nun properly introduced herself...her name was Sister Charles.

Throughout the entire year, she proceeded to be the kindest and most gentle nun I had ever had and would ever have as a teacher in the years to come. While I didn't know it then and apparently was not too wise as to reading clues of future events, she and my Prince Charming shared some things in common. While her kind-heartedness was a partial clue as to how my Prince Charming might behave, I also didn't recognize the clue that was right in front of me. That special nun made the seventh grade the best year of my elementary years. Thank you, Sister Charles!

After graduation, I continued my education in an all-girls, Catholic high school with my latch-key friend. There was no opportunity to see my future Prince Charming...nor any significant other member of the male persuasion. But, after graduation from high school and getting a job to pay for college expenses, I was once again given the opportunity for a princely-sighting. That encounter was not as captivating as the winter, hockey player incident. In fact, that particular meeting had just the opposite effect.

I now worked as a part-time employee at the nearby supermarket, wore a pink and white checkered uniform with a white apron and was called a Checker. I didn't have the luxury of scanning items as they traveled slowly down the conveyer belt. Instead, I had to enter each price onto the keys of what is now considered an antique cash register and pull the lever down to register each item. The hitch was that not every item was marked, and not every Checker had the memory of an elephant with regard to product prices.

I must give credit to the full-time employees who knew the price of every item in the store. How was that even possible? While I thought of those employees as true idols, that particular skill just wasn't in my tool box of grocery techniques. Being a part-time employee, who was not even mildly interested in correcting any product-pricing deficiency, was not entirely conducive to my being on the front lines…the dreaded large order lines.

I was relegated to the short order register in order to do the least harm in aggravating the customers, and even that designation was a misnomer. I was the first to admit that I was slower than a blind turtle crossing a gravel road. But, I was pleasant and polite to the customers, and those qualities were probably the only reasons my employer kept me around.

Until that fateful day, I was content with being the turtle, but everything changed when my Prince Charming walked into the store. Since I hadn't seen him in years, I definitely had to look and act appropriately. I straightened my apron, attempted to look speedy while checking in the items from other customers and gave him my biggest smile as he approached my register. He looked pretty much the same…only older, and might I add, quite handsome with his dark wavy hair and smiling face. I was ready for some possible exchange of friendly banter...perhaps something related to the frosty night of the hockey game and how he noticed me watching from the second-floor window.

What was I even thinking? That fleeting incident was years and years ago, and he just might have been fixing his hat and not really waving to me. My anticipation grew as he approached my counter with a few grocery items. He actually recognized me and spoke of how surprising it was to see me after all of those years. I was delighted that he remembered me, but then the bubble burst...with a bit of an impish grin on his face, he actually referred to my position in the job as being the Chubby Checker!

Did I actually hear him call me a Chubby Checker? The fleeting nostalgia of the hockey game moment went right out of my mind and gave way to righteous indignation. The audacity of this individual to come into my store and exhibit such rudeness. To be fair, I was a bit on the chunky side, was wearing a checkered uniform and called a Checker, but such impertinence was unacceptable. Upon my hearing that remark, I deliberately took my time with his order and was sure to put his bread and tomatoes on the bottom of the bag. He smiled that charming smile of his, mentioned how good it was to see me again and was looking forward to our future encounters at the market...leaving me totally flustered.

Even though my Prince Charming turned into a total toad, he was quite a good-looking toad if I do say so myself.

He never did come into the store again, but each and every time I heard Chubby Checker's hit record of *The Twist*, I thought of my supermarket encounter and forgot about the rude nickname. I only remembered Prince Charming's infectious smile and how I hoped that I would see him again. I was either a total romantic or a complete glutton for punishment!

As fate would have it, years later while in college, I saw my would-be Prince Charming walking down the aisle in the college cafeteria. He looked totally different in that he was wearing a suit, had swapped his curly hair for a crew cut and carried an important-looking, black briefcase. He didn't see me, and I didn't bother to greet him especially after the Chubby Checker incident. (*For the record, I wasn't chubby anymore and considered myself quite fetching!*) However, watching him walk so confidently through the cafeteria reminded me of that extraordinary moment during the winter hockey game of so many years ago. That sentimental thought and the special feeling of the moment made the Chubby Checker comment appear less rude. Instead, his remark seemed quite funny and surprisingly endearing. But, I didn't act on the feelings of the moment by going out of my way to engage in conversation. Instead, I allowed the moment to pass and went about my daily routine. Even though I occasionally looked for him in the cafeteria, I never did see him again while on the college campus.

Once again, years passed. Having graduated from college, I was now working in a public school. After a few years as a teacher, I moved into the office position of Dean of Students. My job involved meetings with students and parents, mediating arguments, arranging staff schedules and quickly re-setting the fire alarms pulled by mischievous, unidentified teenagers. While that particular day seemed like any other day, I was in for quite a surprise…a surprise that would change my life forever.

It was just before the school's dismissal time when the future Prince Charming walked into my office. He was wearing a black trench coat, was impeccably dressed and carried that important looking briefcase. He had given up the crew cut and returned to his previous wavy hair look and was now sporting a rather trendy mustache. For the very first time, I was speechless and for me that was quite a change. What in the world was he doing in my office looking so very cool and confident?

As it turned out, he was a coordinator for a vocational guidance program, and his job involved getting work orders for his teens. The students made metal license plate holders, wooden name plates, business cards and all sorts of products useful for automobiles and offices. He had heard that I was also working in the school system and looked me up in the hopes of my ordering some of the items produced by the students. At least, that was what he told me at the time.

After our conversation regarding potential orders, the business man shifted to his charming personality and inquired if we might pursue our conversation on a social level. The man of my dreams was asking me out on a date…go figure. I checked my non-existent social calendar and agreed there might be some benefit from such an experience.

Truth be told…as he stood in my office and talked about business and social encounters, I had a hunch he was the man I was going to marry. I was finally ready to say goodbye to toads. My Prince Charming was standing right in front of me…

Never again would I experience the thrill of seeing Prince Charming walk into my office after all of those years and ask me for a date. Forget about the Chubby Checker comment. This guy was gorgeous!

When Sparks Fly

In most fairy tales, there is a whirlwind romance complete with laughter, joy and anticipation of the future with every passing moment. Add feelings of longing when the other person is away and pure joy when he or she returns. Sometimes there is an evil force that intrudes on the true romance of the fairy tale, but all events usually work out in the end…in most fairy tales.

Our romance was pretty much the same. The first date was one that I meticulously prepared for in terms of attire. I tried numerous changes of clothes so as to show off my best attributes and dispel the Chubby Checker nickname of years ago. I do believe that I was successful as my Prince Charming's smile of approval was evidence of time well-spent on my dating attire. We went to a popular movie, shared quite a large box of popcorn which I managed to control because I really liked popcorn and ended the special evening with lively conversation at a local pub.

While some might think that sort of date wasn't so spectacular, that evening felt like just a little bit of heaven to me. We talked about all sorts of things…our jobs, ideas, likes and dislikes, and I just didn't want the evening to end.

This man was THE GUY or so I thought…until we got back to my house. As we sat and chatted in his car for a few minutes, he mentioned to me that he knew I was waiting for him to kiss me. What? In that instant, the could-be prince quickly turned back into a distinctive toad! His incorrigible side emerged at a moment's notice and took me totally by surprise. However, I recovered quickly, thanked him for the nice evening and declared that all good things come in time. Leaving him with that thought, I got out of the car and scampered into the house. I only looked back at him once, but the surprised look on his face was worth the fact that I really did want him to kiss me! Somehow, I knew he'd ask me out again. As I mentioned earlier, I was quite fetching, and I could tell that he was intrigued…

Never again would we laugh about our very first date and how much we wanted to share that first kiss. We had such a special evening, and that date was definitely listed in our memories as the greatest first date ever! But, our fairy tale didn't end there. The best was yet to come.

The Courtship

After that first, memorable date, we enjoyed countless dates together. I was never one to appreciate sports, but my Prince Charming had season's tickets to a prominent basketball team in the Chicago area. Many a school night was spent watching those seasoned athletes run from one side of the basketball court to the other. Truth be told, I grew to cherish the events because we were sharing the experience together, and that quality was the charm that made the evenings magical.

He, in turn, ventured into my world by going to plays in the city. One incident in particular that stands out in my mind was the trip to see *The Man of La Mancha* in downtown Chicago. I had planned on taking him to that event and purchased the tickets in advance just so we'd have good seats. As it turned out, my Prince wasn't feeling very well and slept through most of the performance following the intermission. When the play ended, he was awakened by the sound of the applause. I asked him what part of the performance he particularly enjoyed, and he actually gave some plausible explanation as to the events. To be fair, he was really not feeling well but didn't want to cancel going because I had made such special plans. Thank goodness he didn't snore!

    We went to a lot of movies, socialized with friends at some jazz clubs, talked shop about our jobs, played tennis, had similar interests and frequented a Greek restaurant in the city. Because Prince Charming knew the owner, we didn't have to wait in line outside in the cold weather. Being seated immediately at a special table amidst the aroma and danger of the Flaming Saganaki, he and I shared our first dance. That magical moment was offset by the flaming cheese carried by the waiters who served tables bordering the dance floor. Since heavy-duty hair spray was the *in thing* for bouffant hairstyles during that era, the element of danger just made that first dance tremendously memorable.

We learned a lot about each other as the weeks and months flew by. Because we were fairly inseparable when not at our jobs, we somehow decided that marriage was in our future. We didn't have the traditional down-on-one-knee proposal; we just knew we were meant to be together for the rest of our lives. He gave me a gold locket for Christmas that I treasured more than any gift I had ever received.

To this day, that gold locket remains a most cherished gift…

Never again will I experience the feeling from any other gift of jewelry as I did with that gold locket that night. While I received numerous gifts of jewelry for birthdays, holidays and anniversaries throughout the years, none had the heartfelt significance of that treasured locket…on our first Christmas together.

The Wedding

The preparations for the wedding were honestly quite easy as far as I was concerned. My mother, our wedding planner, wanted everything to be perfectly coordinated. Achieving that goal was a bit of a challenge, but she was successful. I truly appreciated her attention to detail from the colors of the flowers to the matching napkins and table cloths. Wedding planning was, indeed, my mother's specialty.

I was fortunate that I fell in love with the first dress I put on and didn't even want to look at any others. When you know in your heart the dress is the right one, you don't look any further. My mother and future mother-in-law also found very beautiful dresses...all coordinated with the colors of the wedding. They both looked beautiful and loved their choices in dresses. The bridesmaids had similar experiences with their choices, so all was well. Without sounding too proud, I was not anywhere close to being a Bridezilla for the wedding. I was actually pretty low keyed. Perhaps I felt that way because I knew in my heart that Prince Charming and I were meant to be together. Thoughts of having wedding jitters never entered my mind.

The only glitch in the wedding plan was that my dear grandmother had suffered a stroke a few weeks earlier and was in the hospital. She was saddened that she wasn't able to attend, but we promised her that we would visit her very soon. My grandmother was so very special to me, and her not being able to attend our wedding was most unfortunate.

The days leading up to the wedding were a bit unusual. My mother, the wedding planner, insisted on having a Groom's Cake. Now, we didn't know what a Groom's Cake was until she told us that it was traditional to give a slice of fruit cake to guests as a token of thanks for coming to the wedding. Prince Charming and I never heard of that tradition but went along with it anyway.

Three days before the wedding, Prince Charming and I traveled by subway train to the downtown area of Chicago and entered the huge basement level of Marshal Field's Department store…now known as Macy's. At that time, the basement of that landmark store held all sorts of delicacies. Now, I never thought of fruit cake as a delicacy nor did I think that there were actually numerous people who ate fruit cakes. I guessed that possibly ten people throughout the United States enjoyed them, and low and behold, my Prince Charming was one of them.

Anyway, we purchased huge loaves of fruit cakes, traveled home and then spent hours cutting the loaves into slices to fit into engraved gift boxes. I have to admit, those gift boxes looked quite special, but the wedding guests were going to get a big surprise when they opened the boxes! However, it pleased my mother that we went along with that tradition, and both of us made a big deal of her wedding-planning expertise. Little did I know that some sort of fruitcake would become a yearly Christmas gift for my dear Prince. Our fruitcake tradition began many years ago with the little box dubbed the Groom's Cake.

All plans fell into place the day of the wedding. The awesome, landmark church was filled with beautiful flowers, and the candlelight service was so meaningful as we took our vows together and became husband and wife. Everything was just so perfect, and Prince Charming and I were finally wed.

Because I was marrying Prince Charming, would I now have the title of princess? I wasn't sure of the protocol, but Prince Charming assured me that he would always treat me like a princess, so having the official title wasn't a necessity. He always had fairly sensible answers for everything.

Rather than have a reception line, we visited my ailing grandmother in the hospital, spent some time with her and gave her my bridal bouquet of brightly-colored flowers. She was both surprised and overjoyed by our visit. Since she was a former dressmaker, we talked about her intricate sewing skills, but her true expertise was evident in the kitchen. Her jam-filled crepes made from scratch on Fridays were worth five-star recognition. She was a culinary wonder in the kitchen and loved every moment of sharing her creations with us. We had such a nice conversation, but we needed to join our guests at the wedding reception. Leaving her was sad, but we were glad to have taken the time to visit with her.

    What we didn't know at the time was that seeing her following our wedding ceremony would be the last time we would see her alive. Knowing that we gave her some small bit of happiness gave us a good deal of consolation in terms of dealing with her loss. She was a very special lady whose daily intention was to make people happy. As far as I was concerned, she always met her goal.

We were excited as we began our journey to the wedding reception. The event was held at a swanky hotel that offered a perfect wedding package. Delicious appetizers were served in the area adjacent to the hotel's pool. Prince Charming and I had bets as to whose school principal would be the first to land in the water. Our administrators had reputations for imbibing large amounts of alcohol, and it was almost inevitable that one or both would land in the pool. However, we both lost those pool-related bets. Perhaps my mother with her unique surveillance techniques had something to do with that…we'll never know.

Everything in the reception area was so well-coordinated, and everyone seemed to have a good time. My mother, who was intent on achieving perfection, was not at all pleased when the gold engraving on the obligatory matchbooks (*Just about everyone smoked cigarettes in those days.*) had Prince Charming's name spelled incorrectly. However, the Prince and I thought the spelling error was a bit funny.

    We shared our first dance as husband and wife to the most popular song of the day...*We've Only Just Begun* by the Carpenters and spent the rest of the evening talking with guests. The event was quite successful, and we had my mother to thank for her efforts.

    Towards the end of the evening, my Prince and I rushed off to begin our new lives together in a glass carriage pulled by a magnificent white stallion. Just kidding! Our vehicle was a 1967, Lime-Gold, Ford Mustang having a black vinyl top with a driver's side door that wouldn't stay closed. As we pulled into this other swanky hotel with the car door held closed with a length of rope, we looked like a couple who had taken a wrong turn and missed the trailer park entrance. But, we didn't care; we were newlyweds and about to begin our life-long journey together…

Never again would I experience the intense, new love I felt for Prince Charming during the wedding ceremony and the beginning of our lives together. Sharing our vows touched my heart in ways I can't describe nor would I even try.

FROM THIS DAY FORWARD

To Have

One might say that we had a lot going for us over the years…lots of *haves*. We had a fairly comfortable life…good jobs, freedom to come and go as our work schedules permitted and a few houses that qualified as money pits. After a few duds in terms of the housing market, we finally had the house that would become our home for years to come, and many exciting adventures awaited us.

During the basketball season, Prince Charming moonlighted as a basketball referee and actually enjoyed the job. The fact that he tolerated the wrath of the spectators always amazed me. Because he had such a gentle nature, how could he withstand that turmoil and verbal abuse from coaches and spectators? All he would say was that he really enjoyed the game as well as being an integral part of it. That was what he had to give to the sport, and I admired his ability to withstand the scrutiny.

On the other hand, I didn't share his passion for the game. Sometimes, I went to his games but hated to hear the anger of the spectators directed at the referees especially since one of them was my easy-going Prince. Well, during one evening of games, I chose a seat in the middle section of the bleachers. Since my appreciation of sports was not the same as the Prince's, I often occupied my time during the earlier games of the evening with the delights of a good book.

On this particular evening, I was so involved in the book I was reading that I failed to realize that people were filling in the bleacher seats around me.

Because spectators frequently traveled up and down the steps of the bleachers, I wasn't paying attention to their movement.

All of a sudden, I was blasted with the sound of trumpets and drums surrounding me with the anthem of the school song. Apparently, the school's Pep Band thought it might be hilarious to quietly surround me while I was reading my book. Their joke was quite the hit with the crowd as they watched my startled awareness of the band surrounding me. When I realized what was happening, I saw Prince Charming looking up at me and smiling at what had happened. As embarrassed as I was, seeing him smile made it all worthwhile.

As a loving couple, we sure had limitless connections going on between us. We had numerous *haves* in our lives…some truly significant and some fairly trivial. Our marriage worked for us, in spite of ups and downs, based upon compromise and commitment. Believe me…having my Prince come home from his basketball game one night without his underwear never gave me a second thought. Maintaining complete trust in each other was, indeed, all part of the *haves* during our entire lives together…

Never again will I see Prince Charming wearing his striped, referee shirt nor will I feel such pride as he performed his duties for the love of the game. His integrity was what made him such a charming prince. He was the total package, and to have him in my life was to have it all!

To Hold

It's not easy to hold onto things, but we managed to make a fairly good attempt at doing just that…especially regarding things that mattered. One thing we always did was hold hands.

I can tell you from the first time he grasped my hand, it felt magical. That sounds much too dramatic, but I immediately experienced such a strong sense of security when his hand held mine. We were on our first date, and he held my hand while helping me in and out of his car. Now, my considerate Prince was indeed a gentleman. His hand was firm yet so soft in cradling mine as I entered and exited his car. This man had style, and even though I had known him since I was an onlooker during his hockey game days of long ago, I definitely needed to learn more about the man he had become.

In the months that followed, I learned a great deal about this man who, as a young boy, played reckless hockey under the tired lights on the city street so many years ago. I just knew that he was the man for me.

He continued to hold my hand firmly each time we went out, entered or exited the car or even when we sat next to each other. We were bound by the holding of the hands and the caring that was the basis for it all. That significant gesture continued for almost forty-five years.

However, the *hold* part of the vows just didn't involve hand holding in social circumstances…it involved much more. Prince Charming held my hand before and after several surgeries as well as cared for me in numerous ways. Our hand holding helped me feel safe during so many difficult situations involving health and everyday living.

Prince Charming did more for me on any given day in terms of assistance through medical situations and life's disappointments. He made my life worth living during the worst circumstances because I trusted the strength of my hand in his. His grasp conveyed the courage I needed to go on…and he made it happen…

Never again will I feel the strength and subtle security each time he held my hand. I will miss that feeling for the rest of my life.

For Better

We had so much fun together. Since our jobs enabled us to have a Spring Break vacation as well as a summer vacation, we entered into the world of time share ownership. Located in picturesque Palm Desert, California, our time share offered the beauty of the desert and created a perfect setting for rest and relaxation. We could either swim in the numerous pools available to us, take short hikes through parts of the desert or join organized tours of nearby attractions. Those weeks spent in the desert resort were so very refreshing to our systems. Each year, we looked forward to the atmosphere of the desert resort as well as the events in the surrounding areas.

As the years passed, we looked forward to a different form of relaxation since retirement was looming in our futures. Our plan was that I would retire first, and my primary job, in my mind, was to do as little as possible. That plan was quite the joke in our household. Having an itemized Bucket List leading with cleaning the basement and organizing the closets seemed appropriate during the pre-retirement months. However, once my retirement commenced, the Bucket List went by the wayside.

I wasn't sure what I would do since I had enjoyed my earlier career and was busy practically every minute of the day while working. There wasn't time for any random strolls through shopping malls or endless watching reruns on the television. But now, I had the world of free time and unlimited opportunities throughout the day at my disposal. Retirement was going to be great!

Aimlessly watching television wasn't entirely satisfying, so I set out to find a project that I was passionate about and could fully dedicate my retirement time to its success. Prince Charming was still working so I took control of household responsibilities with reckless abandon. Laundry was done early in the day, grocery shopping completed by noon, meals were planned and ready for him when he got home from work. The only thing missing was my wearing an apron. I had one that was pretty cute but refused to wear it.

That plan worked for a while, but I still had plenty of time during the day, and I wanted to be useful in some way. As luck would have it, we were having breakfast with some friends, and they mentioned that someone they knew was a puppy raiser for dogs for the disabled. She'd have the puppy for a year, do some basic training, work on appropriate public behavior and then give up the dog at the end of her puppy-raising year. The dog would then go on to advanced training for the disabled.

Since I loved dogs and would only have the puppy for a year, the idea seemed ideal. Our friends put us in touch with this person, and we met her at Brookfield Zoo. The woman was easily recognized because she was accompanied by a magnificent, reddish-brown Labrador Retriever who was wearing a training cape identifying the organization. After talking with her for a while, I was completely hooked on the prospect of being a puppy raiser. Prince Charming wasn't totally on board with my new interest since he was still working. However, he welcomed the opportunity for my trying something new and exciting. Once he and I were officially approved for puppy raising by the organization, the new endeavor was delayed due to a seven month wait for the puppy.

Just before we received our first puppy, Prince Charming led me out to the front of the house where he had purchased and, with the help of a neighbor, positioned a concrete statue of a dog holding a basket of pups. I was overjoyed as to the significance of the statue as well as his determination to make me happy.

The attraction of puppy love was quite strong. Within a few days after receiving that cuddly puppy, Prince Charming was fully on board with the training routine. Together we spent the year watching this puppy grow into a gorgeous dog who was ready and willing to go into advanced training. We, on the other hand, found it most difficult to give up the dog. After giving our first puppy a few kisses and hugs, we reluctantly sent him off with the trainer for his new life without us or more appropriately…our life without him.

We took a few months off and realized that raising a puppy for the organization was very similar to eating potato chips. Can't have just one of them! So, we applied for another puppy and continued this process for fifteen years. One puppy after another crossed our threshold for training, and each puppy became a brief chapter in our lives to be remembered forever.

Our lives just got better and better through our original careers as well as our total commitment to raising these wonderful puppies in retirement. Being best friends with Prince Charming and working closely together was living the dream…

Never again would I see the joy on my Prince Charming's face as he strolled down the street with the young puppy in training, shared his excitement as he taught the puppy a new command or watched him in the quiet moments of the evening with his trusty puppy curled up in his lap. Those moments are lost forever.

For Worse

While we had the usual ups and downs of married life, we thought our lives were pretty typical. We had challenging jobs, lived in a comfortable apartment, made plans for someday buying a house and even getting a dog. We also had the distinct hope of eventually having a family of our own.

Prince Charming loved children and would have made a great father, but our family plan took a bit of a detour…a ten-year detour involving numerous tests and procedures. That alternate, medical route was not at all what we imagined for our lives.

We kept the medical aspect of the numerous tests and procedures private, but we didn't escape the scrutiny and hurtful remarks of family and friends regarding our timeline. They knew nothing of what we were going through, and that lack of personal information was exactly how we wanted to deal with the situation. Sometimes their comments were very insensitive, yet we kept our personal information and issues to ourselves.

Following years of tests, having a family just wasn't in the cards for us. Apparently, that special gift wasn't in the grand design of our lives by the powers that be. We weren't pleased with God's plan by any means and were devastated by what we had to accept in terms of our family plans, but we weren't in any position to dispute the outcome. We had each other, and that bond was all that mattered, or so we thought.

That reversal in our life's plan took its toll in ways that we never thought possible. Our rather perfect life's plans were shattered; and for the first time in our relationship, we weren't equipped to handle the fallout. Perhaps our lives were too easy up until that point which led to our inability to find acceptance as a mutual endeavor that would make us stronger. Instead, our commitment was weakened, and neither of us knew just what to do or how to even begin to fix what was broken.

The entire experience challenged our beliefs in each other and drove a wedge between us. However, through what we knew as our commitment to each other and a lot of help from some very incredible individuals, we were able to find our way back to each other and the promise we made on our wedding day.

Although difficult, acceptance of how our lives changed led us back to what we meant to each other, and that recognition was all that counted. We were truly destined to be together…no matter what happened in the years to come. That realization gave us the courage to move forward and just get on with our lives…

Never again would I dwell on those days during that dark period in our lives. Perhaps that is the only never-again that I won't consider a profound loss. We learned from the experience…our dreams were shattered only to make room for new ones.

For Richer

Riches don't necessarily have to be equated with money and can take the form of many things. As our new lives as husband and wife began, we had a two-bedroom apartment with great, newly-wed neighbors. We resumed our work schedules and began a routine that we both enjoyed.

My energetic Prince enjoyed playing basketball with friends after a busy work-week. I, on the other hand, considered cleaning our apartment to be an enjoyable, therapeutic experience. I would come home from work and rush to our second-floor apartment to begin my detailed process of relaxation through housework. On the way up the stairs, the enticing aroma of garlic and herbs permeating the air would greet me. Unfortunately, it was coming from our neighbor's apartment. She was quite a gourmet cook, and I could only imagine what culinary delights were in the making behind her door.

On the other hand, our apartment projected a very different ambiance. When Prince Charming returned from his weekly basketball game, he would be met with the pungent aromas of the trifecta of cleaning products: Pine Sol, Lysol and Pledge. Believe me, I made full use of the magical solutions and sprays. At times, I was the brunt of jokes from my peers for actually using car wax on the bathroom sinks to avoid water spots. The jokes didn't bother me; cleaning was my form of stress relief, and I took great pride in a job well done! After our Friday rituals, the weekends were ours to devote to whatever endeavors sparked our imaginations.

Our riches included appreciating a loving relationship, having good jobs and enjoying some freedom to travel. Beef wasn't a threat to our well-being, so steaks were frequent dinner items. English Racer bicycles were our main choice of exercise while tennis and even bowling filled some of our free moments. We had it made and often set interesting goals for our summer enjoyment.

The English Racer Marathon was just one of them that unfortunately had a few drawbacks. Because we enjoyed setting goals for ourselves, we decided to train for a type of marathon bike ride…not for a medal or notoriety, but for a cinnamon apple pancake that could be ordered at the Original Pancake House…located fifteen miles away. Since our jobs as educators offered summer vacations, we had the time to train and prepare for the trek. Every other day, we'd increase our mileage to insure our having a successful outing.

The special day of our lengthy journey to pancake heaven finally arrived. The weather was great, and all systems were "Go" for us. We had our path mapped out and knew exactly which streets would get us there safely and in record time. Pedaling down the busy streets gave us an over-all sense of accomplishment; and before we knew it, there it was…The Original Pancake House! While we got to our destination in record time, the anticipation grew as we locked up our bikes and entered the restaurant. The aromas of the regular pancakes on the griddle as well as those of the oven-baked, specialty pancakes filled the air. After placing our order, we relived the experience of setting the goal of getting to the restaurant, training for the trip and actually achieving our bike-riding victory.

The crisp, oven-baked, cinnamon pancakes were finally brought to our table, and the aroma of cinnamon accompanying this lavish breakfast treat was overwhelming. We ate with gusto since the ride to the pancake house was strenuous, and we needed to replenish our energy.

Midway through the meal, it occurred to us that having enjoyed this splendid and filling breakfast, we now had to bicycle back to the house. What were we thinking, and why was this return trip not a consideration in our plan? In hindsight, we might have driven two cars to the pancake house earlier in the morning…left one in a nearby parking lot and driven back to the house before going on our bicycle trek. Then, we might have loaded our bikes into the car after such a satisfying, extraordinary meal and driven home in the comfort of a vehicle. In our enthusiasm and training for the pancake extravaganza, we did not consider the ride back home.

By the time we finally reached our house, we thought those English Racer bicycle seats were permanently embedded in our posteriors. After a period of rest and relaxation, we enjoyed the splendor of our victory. No pain…no gain! However, our marathon bike riding days were over, and we never had the oven-baked, cinnamon pancakes again either.

We also considered humor in our marriage to be a most worthwhile extension of riches. Laughter was an integral part of our day, and an opportunity for a joke or pun might pop up anywhere and often did. On one relaxing vacation to St. Augustine, Florida, my fun-loving Prince toyed with the idea of shaving off his mustache. Even though he asked my opinion many times, I felt that decision was his and his alone. I should have known what was coming next. He came out of the bathroom with the palm of his hand on his face showing only his profile. He asked if I preferred the right side…with the mustache…or the left side…without the mustache. He had shaved half of his mustache off. What a comedian! Love that man!

Prince Charming also didn't care what people thought as he'd often lapse into some Texas drawl while in a Polish Deli or talk about his time share near the Taj Mahal. When on a quest for laughter, nothing phased the man. He accomplished those exploits with total sincerity and a straight face. Nothing was sacred in his world of comedy.

One time in particular, he and a friend jokingly discussed starting a business: a newly-inspired, state-of-the-art Cabousine Transport Service. This high-class, automobile endeavor would provide all the convenience of a cab with the luxury of a limousine. Was there no end to the apparent silliness of these two men? However, common sense prevailed, and thoughts of the Cabousine Transport Service remained silly bantering among friends.

As you might surmise, our days were filled with endless humor. Prince Charming was totally captivated with the songs of the Temptations. They were truly entertainers who brought music to the masses, and I enjoyed them just as much as my Prince did. We often went to their concerts featuring the original group and their songs. Those events were outstanding opportunities for quality entertainment. So much so, that Prince Charming often duplicated their dance movements while in our apartment. One particular incident involved his calling the telephone company for service because he did a triple twirl while holding the phone cord. That magical movement on his part actually led to the phone being pulled from its position on the wall. (*Back in the day, some phones were actually attached to the walls.*) Consequently, a service man from the phone company had to come out to replace the phone as well as fix the hole in the wall.

Was my Prince Charming at the apartment when the representative from the phone company came to put the phone back into the wall? You guessed it. I handled the situation by myself and told the service man that the phone's damaged condition was all due to the triple twirl in the Temptation's song...*Poppa Was A Rolling Stone*! My explanation was given with complete seriousness and without even a hint of laughter in my voice. The telephone service man was not at all amused by my description of the event. He fixed the damaged wall and replaced the dented phone without saying a word. I gathered that he had no knowledge of good music nor did he have a sense of humor.

    We were also richer for having each other's backs when I invited my mother to our apartment for the first time. I had just purchased a Bundt pan and thought its unusual shape was quite interesting. In an effort to impress my mother, I decided to make a sculptured meatloaf in my new Bundt pan. That ingenious twist to the shape of a meatloaf would surely impress her and allow her to believe that I was capable of being a wife who could offer diversity as well as interest to meals.

Knowledge of preparation and timing for this type of endeavor was not in my culinary skill set. As it turned out, I had to chisel away at the lava-like meatloaf in an effort to salvage the meal. By offering numerous appetizers to my mother, the Prince attempted to offset what was eventually coming as the main meal. We salvaged chunks of the meatloaf that didn't resemble lava-rock, placed the edible pieces on a decorative platter with some parsley for garnish and saved the meal.

I had passed the test of a tentative yet successful wife…capable of feeding a male member of the family without the aid of various antacids. By working together, my Prince and I saved the meal.

Our very first Thanksgiving was another test of our ability to feed the masses without any misadventures. Who were we kidding? We actually didn't know that additional turkey drumsticks could be purchased for Thanksgiving dinners without buying another turkey. That lack of culinary expertise led us to stuffing two large turkeys in our rather small oven, and we still didn't have enough drumsticks for our family members!

The situation is funny now, but so very serious at the time in front of family. We truly wanted to make a good impression with our families, but even family members have been known to turn on each other for lack of a drumstick on Thanksgiving.

After our family members left, we had a good laugh about the entire debacle of our first Thanksgiving. We were just so very thankful that we had each other. That was always our fail-safe mode and made us richer for having the security of each other. We also learned a most valuable lesson: turkey drumsticks could be purchased separately…

Never again would I engage in a successful bike-riding marathon with my very best friend, experience the laughter behind his change in dialects in public places nor share the ease of making a rock-solid meatloaf into a gourmet meal to impress my mother. So many never-agains continuously flood my mind. How can I even begin to deal with them?

For Poorer

After two years of apartment living, we decided it was time to go house hunting and discovered an impressive Georgian style house that we considered to be a real bargain. Little did we know that bargains were often pseudonyms for money pits.

We worked every day for two years on that first house of ours and decided that life was just too short to devote so much time to a house. In addition to the daily flow of expenses, someone should have warned us about living across from a school. Since we both worked in the educational field, we should have known better.

After selling the money pit, we were ready to move on to our next housing adventure…new construction. My Prince Charming, driving a rented truck containing numerous items not taken by the movers, looked quite handsome wearing his baseball cap and a slight look of apprehension as he maneuvered the huge vehicle on the crowded highway. Luckily, we arrived at the new house safe and sound, and that element of safety was all that really mattered…except the house of our dreams wasn't finished. Nevertheless, we were young, in love and starting over in a new house. It didn't matter that we had to dodge open air vents and had very limited siding on the house. We really weren't supposed to move in, but we had no place to go. Fortunately, the home inspector kindly allowed us to stay.

Apparently, we were magnets for money pits. Even new construction had its drawbacks. Chasing workers down the street to fix cracked drywall or convincing the village inspectors that we were doing quite well in a house that was clearly in need of bare necessities was an everyday occurrence. However, Prince Charming worked his magic again, and the construction issues were fixed within a few days. This house of ours was finally considered habitable. Way to go Prince!

This particular house, while quite nice, had one serious pitfall: a very small yard and a backyard slope that we dubbed the *suicide slope*. We never saw how steep the slope was on the original plans. It was only when we moved in that we saw the dangers of walking in the yard. We now had two Miniature Schnauzer pups, and even they hugged the grass for safety when let loose in the yard. Mowing the lawn was a risky chore; and as time passed, the challenge became greater and greater.

So, after ten years of defying gravity while either walking or mowing the lawn in the yard, we decided that perhaps it was time to look for a new house. This time, we were going to be smart about our house shopping. We would look for a ranch style house having no *suicide slope* and a larger yard.

Our search began and within a short period of time, we came across a lovely ranch house with a huge back yard. It was the perfect answer to our prayers…or so we thought. No more money pits for us. We were seasoned home owners and knew a bargain when we saw one.

Did we come to this house while riding in the back section of a turnip truck? Was our enthusiasm for a ranch style house with a large yard so overwhelming that we lacked common sense? Apparently, that premise was accurate. We bought the house...well-water and all. We never had that type of water before but thought it might not be all that bad. People survived on well-water. What was the big deal?

Let me tell you, even Prince Charming's charisma could not make the unusual effects of well-water seem wonderful. A representative from the septic system came out to examine the well. We were told that the system had to be shocked. What? We never heard of that technique. Were they going to stand over the well and scream or sneak up on it and scream louder? This event was all so foreign to us. We had to accept that we were once again in unknown territory, and even Prince Charming couldn't get us out of it with his wit and charm.

Well, we did what we had to do; but as time went by, we realized that the gods of the money pit magnets were upon us once again. Too much land, too much well-water, a huge flood in the basement and a furnace that shot flames across the room when turned on made us realize that once again, we were money pit magnets…at the mercy of the housing gods.

However, we didn't lose hope because Prince Charming always had the perfect solution. We would sell this house and design our very own house. We were determined to make this project work for us, and in some ways it did. How much worse could it be? We already experienced two money pits and an unfinished house having a *suicide slope* in the backyard. Since we had the trifecta of housing horrors, our luck was bound to change.

Well, I must admit that this next endeavor turned out to be the house of our dreams. This new construction of our own design was even completed on time and in good condition. This was *THE HOUSE*…the one we would spend the rest of our lives enjoying, and the one we would finally call our home. I did, however, make some changes in later years, but those improvements only added charm to the house…

Never again would I experience the joy of finally having the perfect house. This ranch of our own design would remain lovingly in our hearts and lives for many years to come. After all, it was supposed to be our forever home.

In Sickness

While Prince Charming enjoyed good health throughout most of our married years, things in the wellness department did change for me. I had a series of difficult, structural surgeries that necessitated a lot of assistance. He came through like a champ and over the years helped me through numerous surgeries that involved my feet, knees, both shoulder rotators and ultimately my hand. I almost had enough x-rays to become a skeleton for Halloween!

Most men would have left, but he stayed and helped me through all sorts of fundamental care that would have made some men run for the hills. He only cared about my well-being, prayed for good test results and returned prayers of gratitude when test results were good.

He used to joke that cutting my food for me following rotator and hand surgeries was preparing me for future residence in *The Home*. He sure was a comedian, and the humor he brought to me on a daily basis helped me through some of the toughest times. We had each other, his tremendous ability to make me laugh in the most unusual situations and that mutual sense of security was all that mattered to both of us.

As time passed, Prince Charming experienced some health issues. His running in fundraising races over the years caused some knee problems; and much to his dismay, his chosen running career was sidelined due to a number of surgeries. There were no jokes bantered about in our household regarding this particular loss. He did join me in daily walking, but that endeavor never gave him the same feeling as his running did. Even I couldn't help him with that loss…

Never again would I experience the sincere care and concern given to me by Prince Charming during some of my most painful moments following surgeries, those years of medical tests and intrusive procedures. His prayers for me brought great comfort, and his jokes always took the bite out of the pain. My not being able to help him following the end of his running career was a significant loss for me. He did so much for me in times of illness, yet I wasn't able to return the favor. If we had only known what the future held for us, we might have done things a bit differently.

In Health

In spite of the numerous surgical procedures throughout the years, those health issues were mostly structural and could easily be fixed. The surgeries were certainly inconvenient at the time, but none of the operations necessitated lengthy recuperation periods. All things considered, I felt we were both quite lucky in the health department.

Although what was considered healthy eating changed over time, I prepared what I thought were healthy meals for Prince Charming. Years ago, we enjoyed beef on a regular basis, salads topped with creamy dressings, baked potatoes with butter and even eating bacon on a weekly basis. Salt was a staple for just about every meal and always present on the table. While we didn't know it at the time, those days were definitely soon to become the good old days.

We never grew up with charcoal grilling or even had grills for that matter. I think the closest we came to a grill was a newly-purchased Hibachi that turned on us while on a picnic. We really didn't know what we were doing and never did get the hamburgers cooked that day.

In the dietary department, Prince Charming and I periodically enjoyed hot dogs lined with cheese down the middle, wrapped with bacon and broiled. Who eats like that now? We did back then and enjoyed every delicious morsel of it.

However, age and related health concerns entered the picture. Beef became less frequent, and the broiler never saw those hot dogs again. Salads with light dressing on the side and fresh vegetables became staples in our daily diets. Salt and butter went the way of the dinosaurs. That was okay since we had a good thing going health wise and didn't want anything to change.

My Prince was somewhat free of health issues for a while. Sure, he ate the right foods, exercised every day, ran in races and even ran a marathon due to his endurance and running skills. He was blessed for his efforts by having exceptionally good health.

Yet, there was one exception to his following a healthy diet. His favorite culinary experience was eating a Spam sandwich. That meaty sandwich was served to him for every special occasion that occurred over the years. A sit-down with a Spam sandwich on white bread with pickle relish and mayonnaise was all he needed to be in his gastronomic glory!

The planners of his retirement party offered homage to his special food item by using balloons attached to Spam cans as the centerpieces for the event. Prince Charming was stunned by the thoughtfulness of his co-workers. He was, however, the only one who wanted to take the centerpieces home!

Nevertheless, Prince Charming still maintained a healthy diet in spite of the occasional Spam encounter. Because of his slim stature, I often accused him of being able to sleep on a clothesline. (*Remember those lengths of rope that extended from porch beams that held clothes for drying?*) I also joked about his being able to fit into the pants he wore in high school. I suspected, but wasn't certain, that he still had those in his closet. My Prince was a bit of a pack rat…a very slim pack rat! Even though I joked about his slim stature, I admired his care and concern for his health. He was determined to remain healthy and fit so we could grow old together…

Never again would I watch Prince Charming run in a charity race, prepare for running a marathon, insist on following a healthy diet and passing up everything on the buffet table including French Fries for a salad with dressing on the side. If we were destined to grow old together, I had to follow the same culinary choices. Lots of pressure around that buffet table!

To Love and To Cherish

As we stood before the minister in that quaint church surrounded by family and friends, those two vows were linked together. One did not exist without the other; and while we had our ups and downs throughout the years, we always returned to the significance of those vows.

Prince Charming and I shared such a bond of love that not cherishing each other was never a consideration. From the simplest acts to the significant ones, not a day went by that those emotions weren't shared either quietly or openly in our thoughts as well as in our actions.

We had a few grand displays of those vows in our lives…some more extravagant than others. We were in a position to do things for each other since our jobs offered the element of flexibility that would accommodate occasional grand gestures.

When we planned our wedding, we sacrificed the honeymoon for a wedding scheduled during the Spring Break from our jobs in the educational setting. That week away from our careers would allow us time to get settled in our apartment as well as give us moments to regroup following the wedding festivities.

A week or two following our wedding, my Prince was determined to do something special for the upcoming, holiday weekend. The preparations included his making our most favorite drink...the Manhattan. Before we were married, he had moonlighted as a bartender for a fancy catering service so his knowledge of mixology was right on track.

Making the perfect Manhattan was his goal. Let me tell you that after a few attempts, he reached perfection in terms of the proper combinations. But, the festivities didn't end there. Since we were now beginning a lengthy holiday weekend, we needed a way to celebrate this momentous Manhattan occasion. Taking a trip to a special place was the answer.

By the afternoon of the next day, we were appreciating the glorious atmosphere of Paradise Island in the Bahamas. You can't beat that! We had great weather for the entire weekend. Prince Charming's attempt to impress me by making a triple summersault in three feet of water and incurring a huge abrasion on his shoulder was, indeed, unfortunate. In spite of the horrendous sunburns sustained by each of us, going back to our jobs on Tuesday was somewhat uncomfortable, but we still considered the weekend to be a great success. Even after all of these years, that spur-of-the-moment, celebratory trip remains a truly romantic gesture.

Prince Charming always thought of me as special. I valued that delusion on his part and constantly fostered the misconception because it worked in my favor. Just kidding. We were actually very special to each other, but I really played into his biased thoughts about me and couldn't stop myself from encouraging them!

Following a very challenging series of weeks at my job, Prince Charming had planned a surprise holiday weekend away from the pressures of work. He contacted my school principal with a request for my taking some personal days off, planned the trip and actually packed my clothes and his for the weekend. At dismissal time, he met me at my school and whisked me away to the airport. Within a few hours, we were landing in Tampa, Florida. He had planned the entire surprise by himself…just because I was struggling with my job, and he wanted to make things easier for me. Making that happen was a perfect example of those vows…to love and to cherish.

However, my Prince wasn't the only person in our marriage who planned occasional grand gestures. He was an avid sports fan and especially enjoyed watching the games played by the Chicago White Sox baseball team on television. Following a very stressful time in our relationship (*Yes, we had them, and they were doozies.*), I wanted to do something special for him that was exceptionally fulfilling in terms of his love of sports. Since Prince Charming was quite the baseball enthusiast, I found information about the fantasy baseball camps that were emerging around the country. I was especially interested in the Cubs Fantasy Baseball Camp in Arizona.

Now, this was a Chicago Cubs Baseball Camp, and my husband was a White Sox fan. Are you sensing the irony? Truth be told, there was never anything sinister in the choice. The White Sox camp hadn't been well-established at that point, and I wanted a camp with a reputation for offering the best of experiences. I made all of the surprise arrangements that involved requesting special permission from his school administrator, sent his uniform size to the camp organizer, made the airline arrangements as well as created a framed invitation to attend the camp.

For the very first time in our relationship, my Prince was speechless. It was a dream come true for him…a week spending time with former players of the Chicago Cubs and actually participating in games with them. What was not to enjoy?

I didn't want to intrude on the men's good times, so I didn't go to the camp until the end of the week. The campers were playing an official game in a huge stadium against the former players of the Cubs. The event was so exciting! Seeing my Prince wearing the uniform of the Chicago Cubs with kids asking for his autograph before the start of the game was truly an awesome experience.

Prince Charming pitched a very good game, received his own personal baseball cards as a player and enjoyed the most unforgettable baseball team experience. That fantasy baseball camp week was probably the next best week in terms of great memories following our wedding. I was so happy to have provided that gift for him.

As we approached our thirtieth wedding anniversary, Prince Charming suggested that I plan something to mark the significance of that date. I was usually one to color within the lines of decorum until my dentist suggested something very unique during my scheduled visit. He mentioned that his sister had a most incredible experience as she and her husband approached a significant wedding anniversary.

I listened to his description of her experience, did some research on the suggestion and decided that for once, I would do something totally outside the outlines of my upbringing. I planned the renewal of our vows to take place at the Graceland Chapel in Las Vegas with an Elvis impersonator! Now, I was sure that event might raise some eyebrows as to the inherent possibility for irreverence, but I went ahead and made the plans anyway.

To say Prince Charming was taken aback by my plans was definitely an understatement. But, the plans were made, my latch-key friend and her husband were going with us as matron of honor and best man, and together we would share a unique and adventurous experience.

Needless to say, the sparkling clean limousine that picked us up at the hotel, the gorgeous flowers that I had chosen and the elegance of the quaint chapel with its colorful, stained-glass windows removed any thoughts of irreverence for the event. The Elvis impersonator, a most handsome hunk of an individual, looked and dressed like the young Elvis. While he shared a bit of levity during the ceremony, nothing was lacking in taste. During his songs, his voice resonated with such clarity that if one closed one's eyes, the authentic Elvis was actually singing those beautiful songs.

The total experience from start to finish wasn't at all tacky as one might first imagine…especially with a chapel surrounded on both sides by Bail Bond establishments. Even the photographer, who took incredible photos, was extremely professional in that she stopped traffic on the boulevard so cars wouldn't be in our group photos. This experience was so well-organized and tasteful that it remains one of the best grand gestures in our marriage.

However, grand gestures were actually few and far between in our relationship. The daily expressions of to love and to cherish filled our lives in either small or big ways throughout our marriage.

The day-to-day things we did together throughout the years probably seemed a bit dull to others. Sharing secrets, sitting beside each other in church knowing that we were praying for each other's well-being, going to movies, watching television together and knowing that we were each other's best friends meant everything to us. Those events described our real lives together.

My Prince was a gentleman in every sense of the word. Opening doors for me, holding my hand when out in public or giving me a surprise hug or kiss was just the norm for him. Bringing flowers to me for no special occasion was one of his favorite gestures.

However, he never failed to bring me flowers on the anniversary of our first date. Prince Charming's actions on a daily basis reminded me of how much to love and to cherish held profound significance in our lives.

I, on the other hand, did the same in other ways. When out with the ladies for our monthly lunch dates, I always made sure to bring home a special dessert for him from the dessert bar. Preparing his favorite meal as a surprise was just a reminder of how much I cared for him or the simplest act of buying goofy socks for him that had the correct foot designation on them as a joke brought out the laughter that was so much a part of our lives.

Sure, we had our ups and downs and often expressed being sorry for some gesture of irritation over a silly act. I, more so, than he said those words a lot. But, we never let a day go by with anger hanging over our heads. Never going to sleep angry and always wishing him safe travels when he left the house for errands or to meet friends were standard procedures.

We couldn't even imagine our lives without each other's kindness, consideration and laughter that became the credo of loving and cherishing we offered each other on a daily basis. Our years together weren't endured, they were enjoyed to the fullest…

Never again will I hear his laughter, return his hugs, see his vibrant smile or experience quite so many treasured, loving acts that he gave me every day of our lives together. How does one survive the loss of so many never-agains?

Until Death Do Us Part

The solemn cadence of the ventilator was closely reminiscent of a metronome counting out the concise beats to music. However, this particular machine wasn't counting out musical beats. Instead, this vital mechanism was counting out breaths of life…my dear Prince Charming's life.

As I sat next to his bed in quiet disbelief, the coolness of the Cardiac Intensive Care Unit was contributing to the numbness that had taken over my body. While attempting to process the preceding events, I asked myself how we got to this place, and why was this even happening? It wasn't supposed to happen!

All I remembered was walking out of Prince Charming's room into the hall and suddenly hearing the sound of the words *Code Blue* over the intercom. Doctors and nurses rushed from rooms I never even knew existed and hurried into Prince Charming's room. At that very moment, a cold shiver filled my body accompanied by feelings of dread. In that instant as I reached for a chair to steady myself, I knew with utmost certainty that barring a miracle, my beloved Prince would never leave that hospital alive.

    I quickly followed behind the gurney carrying my cherished Prince Charming to the Cardiac Intensive Care Unit and hoped beyond hope that my feelings of dread were premature. I had to hope that everything was going to be okay, but the chilled numbness that filled my body told me otherwise.

    Those horrible events led us to this moment in time. Lulled by the beeping of the monitors and the steady cadence of the ventilator, I looked around the room for some strategic point of reference...something that might help me understand what had happened and the reasons why we were here in this cold, machine-filled room.

Surrounded by numerous bags of intravenous medicines hanging from stands that formed a fence-like barrier around my dear Prince, I sat in total disbelief over the events that had just occurred. Even though connected to numerous machines, he looked a bit relaxed or as relaxed as one might be with wires attached everywhere on one's body. If only he would wake up for even an instant, it would signal a glimmer of hope for his recovery. He looked so very peaceful in the cold climate of the room. I wondered if he felt the cold as I did and wondered what comfort I might offer.

Being a very religious individual, Prince Charming always carried a small wooden cross in the side pocket of his jacket. As I went to hang up his jacket, his wooden cross fell to the floor from the pocket. Seeing the cross as a sign of hope, I picked it up, gently placed it in his hand with my hand over his while praying and hoping for a miracle. If anyone deserved a miracle, my Prince did. He never hurt anyone, never spoke ill of others and always found the good in people even if they offended him in some way. He needed this miracle and required it as soon as possible.

I called upon God, the Blessed Virgin Mary and every saint I knew for help with Prince Charming's condition. I pleaded, bargained, bartered, offered to do anything…even switch places with him…just so he would recover and be well again. But, I guess the prayer lines were busy that night. I'm told that God answers all of our prayers, but sometimes his answer is *No*. Since Prince Charming wasn't waking up, I knew what God's answer was.

So, I sat quietly with my Prince, read to him every hour from his favorite book, talked to him about our lives together and continued to pray with his wooden cross clutched in his hand surrounded by mine. We were even holding hands in the Cardiac Intensive Care Unit hoping our love for each other would make a difference. Maybe the prayer lines weren't as busy in the middle of the night. One could always hope for that to occur, and someone of higher authority might answer. Hope was all I had at this point, and I continued to pray.

As the night progressed, meds were changed, Prince Charming's vitals were checked, but there was still no response in terms of waking up. Staring at the man who was the love of my life and not being able to do anything to help him was agonizing. Once again, I asked myself how did we get here, and why was this terrible event happening? I had to find some reasons for this horrible situation.

Sitting in a hospital recliner next to Prince Charming's bed, I began to recreate the happenings of this terrible day as well as backtrack through the days, weeks and months that led to this moment. It was months ago that my Prince was given a diagnosis of triple forms of cancer. We called them The Three Amigos. Two were easily treated, but one in particular was the tricky one…the advanced condition that wasn't detected in any physicals or advanced testing the year before…so much for the credibility of modern medicine.

Because we were given numerous assurances that each was treatable, we attempted to deal with The Three Amigos as horrible inconveniences and hoped specialized treatments would rid Prince Charming of them in time. There was optimism in every day, test and treatment. So, I asked myself, why were we here now in this cold, sterile room hoping for a miracle? No answers came; there were no voices from above, and no soothing words of consolation offered…only the steady sound of the ventilator challenging the silence of the room in the middle of the night.

Still, I wondered…what led to this moment in time? Were the weeks of dreadful chemotherapy responsible for my Prince's weakened immune system? Was his condition due to the extended delay and total incompetence exhibited by staff in the emergency room, the lack of having appropriate pain medication available or the blatant nonchalance of medical personnel? Something was the cause, or someone needed to take responsibility for my beloved Prince Charming's condition. But, no one stepped forward with answers or accountability…just the sound of the ventilator filled the room.

    That morning, our favorite priest came to visit and offered words of consolation to me and administered the Last Rites to Prince Charming in case he wasn't able to bring himself out of the deep sleep that enveloped him. Friends came to offer support and prayers. Perhaps their lines of communication had better reception with God than mine. Still, the lines remained busy, and all prayers went unanswered.

As a last resort, and I'll admit it was a shallow attempt, I opted for fear tactics. I moved closer to my soulmate and softly whispered into Prince Charming's ear that if he didn't wake up, I would be in charge of the check book. To this date, I had never ever balanced the checkbook in our entire relationship. If seen with the checkbook in my hands, fear would overcome Prince Charming as his record of success in monthly balancing was in jeopardy. I really thought that threat would wake him up, but my fear tactic went unnoticed. That fact signaled very deep trouble as well as unleashed the fear that had been hidden within me for the past few days.

To onlookers, the numbness and machine-like mode that directed me through the days must have seemed unusual for someone facing all of the stress and emotions involved with the situation. However, what onlookers didn't know was that my Prince and I had a pact. If ever one of us were facing distressing circumstances, the other one had to remain calm in order to make informed decisions when the other one couldn't. This crisis was my turn to remain calm, and it was proving to be the most difficult task I had ever faced. I wanted to scream, to cry and to sob for my Prince Charming's situation, but I knew two things were very certain: I made a pact that I knew I had to keep for his sake, and the other was that if I started to cry, I would never stop. I would be of no assistance to my dear Prince if that happened.

Another day went by with few interruptions except for the muted echoes of the machines...now as unnoticed as background music in elevators. Doctors and nurses came and went in silent processions at various times of the day, checked monitors and changed medications. I still read to my Prince from his favorite book every hour and spent a lot of time talking about our lives together.

Then, I thought that perhaps Prince Charming might be fearful on some level of being in this cold and sterile room while hooked up to all sorts of machines. In an effort to lessen those fears, I resorted to a tactic used when we had a new puppy who might be frightened of being alone in a new environment. I would hold the pup in my arms and sing the first verse of the song...*You Are My Sunshine*. The song seemed to work every time with the pups. However, when I tried it with Prince Charming, I barely made it through the relevant lyrics because of the extreme emotion of the situation. That realization signaled what I had refused to allow in my thoughts…I was going to lose my Prince Charming of almost forty-five years. My sunshine was being taken away, and there was nothing I could do about it.

A few days passed, and Prince Charming's condition in terms of not waking up remained the same, but other significant health issues were creeping into his condition. Infection was of great concern as well as the potential for another episode of cardiac arrest. I needed more information from the doctors in order to make informed decisions…decisions I didn't want to make. Numerous doctors gave their opinions, and none were even tinged with a bit of hope for my Prince's recovery. Much too much damage had occurred, and The Three Amigos were winning this battle.

After considerable soul-searching in terms of what was the best decision to make for my best friend in the entire world, I came to the painful decision to allow his sleep to continue without the assistance of the ventilator's cadence sustaining his life. Sitting with him, reading to him and sharing those last moments of his life will be etched in my mind and heart for the rest of my life.

Amidst the newly attained silence of the room without the machines, Prince Charming quietly slipped away from me and our lives together. As I removed his wedding band from his finger, he looked at peace for the first time in days. I kissed him for the very last time…saying my final good-bye to him and to the end of our fairy tale. We had a successful run as fairy tales go…just not long enough as far as I was concerned…

Never again will I experience the magical life shared with my Prince Charming, my soulmate and best friend. Seeing his smiles, hearing his laughter, feeling the comfort of my hand in his, enjoying the security of his hugs as well as all the wonderful moments we shared are all gone forever. How does one endure such profound losses when the heart is broken?

AFTER THE FAIRY TALE ENDS

The Journey Begins

Time seemed to stand still in the moments following the silence of life drifting away. While sitting beside my Prince Charming, I wondered if he were now free from pain and suffering. What was next for me without him in my life?

Remembering our pact reminded me to remain calm in the face of adversity and deal with the intense pain of loss. After saying my last goodbye to the wonderful man who filled me with joy every day of our lives, I once again forced myself into a machine-like mode. Papers had to be signed, decisions made and plans formulated.

When all of the paperwork was completed, I slowly made my way to the valet station in order to get my car. I knew it would take a while because the car had been in the hospital's back lot for days, so I just stood waiting in the outer doorway. While I didn't notice people around me, I did see that snow had fallen heavily during the day. The cars in the parking lot seemed to vanish under the heavy blanket of fallen snow…giving the lot the aspect of emptiness. My life was now as empty as the appearance of the snow-covered lot. The one person who made my life complete was gone, and I had no idea how I would or could face that reality once I gave in to the emotion of the situation.

As the driver arrived with my car that he had kindly cleared of snow, he mentioned how wonderful everything looked with the newly-fallen snow. Could he tell that I was lost in thoughts of what had just happened? All I could do was nod, thank him for his kindness and hope that no more conversation was necessary. I needed to get home so I could face this situation with the emotion I had hidden deep in my body for months. This last day and those final moments would remain in my mind forever. Thankfully, the gentleman just helped me into the car and allowed me to leave the parking lot without any further conversation.

Driving home through the snow-laden streets, thoughts of the last few days rumbled around my mind. I concluded that these events were all part of a horrible nightmare that took hold of my night's sleep. Soon my Prince would be shaking me awake from the terrors as he had done in the past when my nightmares occurred.

I had frequent nightmares all relating to my childhood home in the city. I'd dream of walking through the pitch-black gangways at night as well as having the responsibility of going down open-sided stairs in the dark to the basement level to make sure all doors were closed and locked. The nightmares were always the same, but my Prince would wake me from the horrible experiences that filled my dreams. All I had to do was get home and await Prince Charming gently bringing me back to reality.

As I pulled into the driveway of our home, I saw the quaint porchlights that we picked out together and entered the darkened house that was devoid of all sound. Now, I knew no one was going to wake me up ever again. Prince Charming's passing was real, and this horrible happening wasn't a dream at all. This stark realization was one of many never-agains that I would face in the days ahead.

At last, I gave myself permission to cry for the loss of my soulmate, best friend and love of my life. As I sat in the darkness of our sunroom, curled up in his favorite wicker chair, tears flowed for hours. The room faced the snow-covered yard full of endless memories of our times together. I smiled just a bit when remembering Prince Charming's cutting of the electrical cords connected to the garden trimmer. According to him, the responsibility for the damaged cords on three occasions was due to his being left-handed. He used that excuse a lot, but remembering his defense only made me smile a bit more. After those cord-cutting episodes, I became his trusty assistant in charge of holding the cords…away from the bushes being trimmed and shaped.

Seeing the huge spruce tree in the backyard, heavily laden with snow, reminded me of the gorgeous pear tree that occupied that space years ago. Because we purchased the tree for our fifteenth wedding anniversary, we officially named it our Anniversary Tree. Each year on our anniversary, we sat beneath the pear tree's branches on a wooden bench and celebrated another year together.

When a terrible storm ripped through the neighborhood a few years ago, our Anniversary Tree fell victim to the ravages of the wind and rain. Even though a tall spruce tree now stood in our special tree's place, I still pictured us sitting on that bench under our Anniversary Tree. We were so happy back then, and now everything in our lives had changed.

At some point during the night, I felt myself sobbing uncontrollably for the unbelievable loss. My heart actually ached, and I wondered if this pain were what a broken heart felt like. I knew people actually died of a broken heart and wondered if this was the fate that awaited me. The very thought of that happening was somewhat comforting in a strange way.

    Then, I looked around the room and saw all of the bundled, unopened mail collected during the hospital stay as well as the disarray of the house. Since my trips back and forth to the house were rushed, I made no attempts at neatness. With those thoughts in mind, I realized that my responsibilities as Prince Charming's wife were definitely not finished. I had friends to notify, arrangements to make and a memorial service to plan. Government agencies and numerous other groups had to be informed of his sudden passing.

Prince Charming handled all of the finances so that, in itself, was a major obstacle as well as a challenge for me. Then, I saw the dreaded, bulging manila envelope that contained a task way beyond my skill set...income tax information. I was in big trouble since I held the record for never balancing a checkbook in almost forty-five years. The thought of having to do the income tax was all too overwhelming to even imagine. That admission on my part was quite pitiful, but Prince Charming insisted on handling all of the issues regarding finances. He actually enjoyed every single moment dedicated to that endeavor since he had a background in banking.

All of those responsibilities as well as numerous problems not even anticipated meant that dying of a broken heart would have to wait. I had to put everything in order and clean the house before that option was a serious consideration or even a possibility. I might not have been involved in the financial aspect of our marriage, but I had a reputation for having a very clean and dust-free house…

Never again will my Prince Charming and I share wonderful moments together in our sunroom. Looking out at the snow-covered yard, I felt such emptiness and couldn't even imagine my life without him. He was my strength and courage in all aspects of our life together. How will I ever manage without him?

Reality Sets In

Morning came quickly, and I realized that not only was I still sitting in his favorite wicker chair looking out at the yard, but I was also still wearing my winter coat that I failed to remove when getting home from the hospital. I was drained from the crying but knew that in the absence of my immediate family's assistance, my latch-key friend was ready and willing to take their place. She would be at my side and be supportive in everything I needed to do for my Prince's final arrangements. Her being with me was a tremendous emotional support since I wasn't sure if I could manage my machine-like mode for everything necessary in the days to come.

As methodically as we could, she and I went from place to place making final arrangements. I had to take my thoughts out of the emotional level and not even dare think about this horrible loss. If I focused on the loss and allowed myself to grieve, there was no turning back to making reasonable decisions. Remembering our pact regarding one of us being in control during a crisis kept me in that decision-making mode. Since we adhered to that agreement for almost forty-five years, I forced myself into that state of mind where decisions were made rationally.

With the arrangements made, the next step included the preparations for Prince Charming's memorial service. I arranged for our favorite priest to preside, mementoes had to be gathered and picture boards created. Arranging for the priest to preside was relatively easy since he was a good friend to us. On the other hand, organizing the mementoes and picture boards caused highly emotional responses.

Choosing the pictures for the display boards was laden with tears of both joy and sadness. Seeing him in such happy circumstances in pictures, regretting never seeing him do the things he loved again and ultimately, feeling not one bit of hope for the future was terribly disheartening.

Selecting the showcase for Prince Charming's racing medals, arranging for a proper display of his Chicago Cubs' uniform as well as finding a suitable presentation stand for the jacket and hat of his favorite hockey team, the Montreal Canadiens, was next on the list of things to do. These items meant so much to him, and I needed to find just the right way to show them to his friends at the memorial service.

One delivery, in particular, that pulled me out of my robotic-mode into full-fledged sobs, was a gift from the doctors and staff of the animal hospital that treated all of the pups we raised for potential service. The floral delivery contained white lilies surrounded by greenery, but the inscription on the vase caused me to break down all over again. The engraving read…*In memory of a life most beautifully lived*.

Those members of the animal hospital staff were firsthand witnesses of my Prince's goodness over a period of almost fifteen years and sent something so very significant in terms of honoring his life. I not only included the vase in the memorial service but would display it in a special place in our home for the rest of my life. Prince Charming will never be forgotten for the beautiful life he lived.

I know memorial services are referred to as A Celebration of Life, but I just don't get it, nor do I accept the concept. In accordance with proper etiquette, I planned the event and knew that Prince Charming's friends would look upon it as a celebration of his life...a life lived in goodness and kindness, but he was gone from my life forever.

In all honesty, I refused to honor him in that manner. His life was with me; and while I will grieve for his loss every day for the rest of my life, I refused to consider this memorial a celebration...

Never again will I watch my Prince Charming running in his charity races, smiling as he did in all of the

pictures displayed throughout the memorial setting, nor will I see him proudly wearing the flame-red jacket and hat of his favorite hockey team…the Montreal Canadiens. Those never-agains were all just so difficult to accept.

I hoped that I might return to the idea of this entire event as being a horrible, extended nightmare, but I knew the real nightmares were yet to come. This unthinkable loss was real, and I wasn't sure I could handle it…in spite of the pact I made with Prince Charming in much happier times.

Prince Charming Remembered

All the plans for the memorial service were made, and many thanks were once again offered to my latch-key friend whose own family was gradually becoming my surrogate family. As the day approached for the memorial, I had worries that I wouldn't be able to go through with the service. How was I supposed to greet people, be grateful for their coming as well as sharing moments of Prince Charming's life without totally breaking down from the extreme loss?

The night before the service, I refused to sleep because I needed to find the courage to go through with this memorial called a Celebration of Life. I didn't believe this memorial was anywhere close to a celebration, but I was an integral part of the service whether I agreed with the concept or not. I had to gather the courage to do this for him. While staring into the darkness of the yard, I spent the night nestled in his favorite wicker chair in the sunroom waiting for the sun to rise.

The morning of the memorial service, I somehow found the necessary courage to do what I had to do for my Prince. My latch-key friend picked me up at the scheduled time, and other good friends met us at the memorial site to help with setting up the various remembrances of Prince Charming's wonderful life.

As guests arrived, I greeted them as best as possible and listened to individuals share wonderful stories of the impact Prince Charming had on their lives. Current as well as past friends spoke of his goodness and kindness. Former students from his past guidance counselor position shared memories of the wonderful influence he had on their lives. Puppy raisers came with their young dogs-in-training to acknowledge the role he had in raising puppies for the sake of the disabled. So many people from all walks of life celebrated his life and yet, I couldn't do that for him. I refused to rejoice in his passing as the memorial continued.

Our favorite priest spoke so eloquently about Prince Charming's strength, kindness and compassion for others. Friends shared sensitive as well as numerous, humorous anecdotes of his life…mostly humorous since he was known for that special side of his personality. Finally, the priest sang what he considered a tribute to my dear Prince's passing and his new life with God. I remember sitting there listening to his beautiful song and wondering why this was considered a celebration. Prince Charming was gone, and the fairy tale was over.

The service ended, people left for the celebratory luncheon and following that event, only my friends stayed to help with gathering all of the keepsakes of Prince Charming's life. Thankfully, my friends were there to help me put the pieces of my Prince's life back together for the last time and his final journey home. Their assistance was gratefully appreciated.

After all was brought into the house, the beautiful flowers were taken to the Catholic Church, the picture boards were stacked in a special room as were Prince Charming's favorite Montreal Canadiens' jacket and hat. His uniform from the Chicago Cubs Fantasy Camp was put into the closet as well as all mementoes of our wedding. Only framed pictures of him remained throughout the house as well as the cherished vase that meant so much to me from the animal hospital's staff. I was now facing being alone in a silent house that was once our loving home.

The memorial was over, and my friends, who were reluctant to leave me alone, left at my insistence. I was there in our house with only his memory of a life so beautifully lived. How would I ever be able to live through this unbelievable sadness much less face my empty life? More importantly, I wasn't sure I even wanted to survive this unimaginable loss. My aching heart felt broken, and I wasn't sure that moving forward was the way to heal that damage...

Never again will I feel the comfort that sharing my life with Prince Charming provided. Hearing his friends share touching memories of him was heartwarming, but I knew that I was broken inside, and nothing would ever fix me.

Grief Galore

Grief has a very unsettling and spontaneous way of manifesting itself on those who suffer the loss of a loved one. The element of surprise was the ace in the playing cards held by Grief, and those unkind surprises come in the form of something called triggers. Although others may view them differently, I considered the triggers to be nasty prompts that latched onto the memories or never-agains of my life and increased the intensity of sadness. Springing up in the most unusual places, those dreadful triggers caused such extreme pain, heartache and tears. Grief's art of incurring emotional pain and setbacks with even the smallest of triggers was an ongoing threat to my well-being.

My triggers materialized in the most unusual places. The first and quite unexpected trigger, aside from the sadness and tears that dominated my daily life, occurred in the most unlikely place...the grocery store. Having a schedule was important to me in order to maintain some sort of life with the living. So, going to the grocery store was a field trip for me...some place to get me out of the house wearing clean clothes and makeup. I was serious about following a set regimen of care as opposed to staying in bed all day long.

As I aimlessly ventured from aisle to aisle, all was well until I came to the frozen food section. When I stopped at the vegetable section and opened the door of the freezer, I viewed the frozen packages of broccoli neatly stacked on the shelves. Prince Charming loved his broccoli, and I often filled our freezer with bags of his favorite veggie. Grief barged in with its surprise trigger, and I found myself in tears staring at those bags of broccoli. Why was I crying, and why couldn't I close that door of the freezer? I, unintentionally, drew some attention to myself because onlookers didn't know why I was crying while standing in front of bags of frozen broccoli. I just stood there, as frozen as those bags of vegetables, thinking that closing the door would mean losing my Prince again.

I finally brought myself back to reality and closed the completely clouded door of the freezer. My Prince was gone, and frozen broccoli had nothing to do with my loss. Some people just gave me strange looks, but at that point, I didn't care. I just needed to get back to the house. I left the store without my groceries, and halfway home, I realized that Grief had won that hand. It played the frozen food card and won…hands down!

Grief often sent numerous other triggers…springing up at all times during the day. While shopping in a crowded department store, the scent of Prince Charming's favorite cologne filled the air as a gentleman passed me by, and once again, I lost that hand to Grief. So many memories filled that brief encounter with the aroma of that special cologne, and yet I couldn't control my response. I had to leave the store since the extreme sadness was not going to allow me to accomplish anything. Grief had the triggers and knew what would spin me off into my past fairy tale. There was no fairness in this fight, and I was not armed with any possible defense against the sadness and the tears that overcame me when the triggers struck.

One of my worst experiences with those surprising triggers occurred as I approached the malt shop that had options for the most wonderful vanilla, chocolate and strawberry malts on their menu. Prince Charming craved and was able to consume those flavorful malts while undergoing his chemotherapy treatments. Those luxurious ice cream delights not only soothed his troubled mouth from the side effects of chemotherapy but somehow, filled his spirit with hope that things would get better. Each day, I ventured to that shop to get the favorite malts for my Prince; and each day, I was filled with new hope that all would be better. Ice cream was supposed to make things better, wasn't it?

Weeks after Prince Charming had passed away, I was driving past the malt shop and immediately felt the triggers of Grief once again working against me. I had driven by that shop many times after my Prince had passed away, but this particular time was different. As I reached the stop light near the ice cream shop, I suddenly felt a tightness in my chest as the anxiety increased. The tears came so fast that I wasn't able to even see the road clearly. I pulled off to the shoulder of the road and just sobbed until my ribs ached. Prince Charming would never enjoy his favorite malts again, and I had no hope of ever seeing the comfort those extra-thick vanilla, chocolate and strawberry malts gave him while enduring those horrible treatments.

It was then that I decided that Grief had no boundaries in terms of inflicting pain and suffering. My fight with Grief wasn't a fair one and never would be...I had already lost the battle when Prince Charming passed away.

There were many other triggers in my daily life associated with memories that would spring up unexpectedly...a laugh heard in a group sounding like my Prince Charming's, selecting two plates for dinner instead of one or seeing a man of similar stature wearing a baseball cap running past the house. Sometimes watching a loving couple holding hands in the park, hearing a special song on the radio, glancing at his favorite recliner and imagining him sitting there or something as simple as seeing a pothole in the street would send me running for tissue. Sad to say, my sweet Prince was a huge magnet for potholes...if one lurked somewhere in the street, he would find it.

Such simple things had the power to either lead me to the side of the road until the tears stopped or send me to his favorite wicker chair for consolation. Everything we shared together would remain targets for those nasty triggers. Grief was ruthless in terms of depriving me of any form of peace to enter my life.

I had to face the fact that Grief's triggers were designed to pop up everywhere…no matter how hard I tried to avoid them. Since Grief had no limitations when it came to inflicting heartache, I had to forge on with my life without Prince Charming in spite of Grief's interference. As far as I was concerned, moving forward was easier said than done. Grief held the upper hand and would probably have some form of control over me for the rest of my life.

I still had a lot of things in the household to settle. I had only balanced the checkbook once in the months since Prince Charming's passing. That was not the greatest of records, but it was the best I could accomplish under the circumstances. I did a limited version of my *Happy Dance* in front of my Prince's photograph to celebrate the one-time happening. As sad as reveling in the balancing of the checkbook might seem, my winning that battle was truly an event to be recognized. I also believed that Prince Charming was celebrating as well. I was certain that wherever he was in God's hierarchy, he was just as surprised as I was…

Never again would I forget the immense power of Grief's unpredictable and annoying triggers

lurking in everything my Prince Charming and I shared. They would, undoubtedly, remain with me forever. Nor could I ignore the sadness that snuck into my thoughts when remembering special places he and I traveled through the years. I just had to face Grief's unwanted triggers and move forward. Was doing that even possible? Most days, I didn't think it was.

Family Is Just A Concept

Depending on the individual or the situation, the concept of the word *family* varies. To some, the concept of *family* means the bonding together of individuals through birth. To others, the notion of *family* takes on an entirely different perspective.

In my current state of turmoil, I had hoped that whatever birth family issues of the past that had transpired and alienated us from each other would take the back seat to my grief. I needed the special support that came only from birth connections to help me through the worst possible moments in my life. Sadly, that type of familial support was not forthcoming, and at the risk of sounding ever so dramatic, I really felt totally abandoned by my family. Their presence at my dear Prince Charming's memorial service was the last time I saw them nor have I heard from them in the eight months since that extremely unhappy occasion.

Periodically, I'd ask myself, how does one not keep in contact with a relative in light of the pain of grief? In fairness to them, I was sure they had some reason to be absent from my life at this time; I just wish I had known what that reason might have been. In knowing, we might have had an opportunity to make things right or at least to try…but, we'll never know unless something changes in the future.

Consequently, my concept of family turned to friends who were there when I needed them the most. Those individuals who dropped everything that day to rush to the Cardiac Intensive Care Unit to sit with me while waiting for some sign of change in Prince

Charming's condition. His best friend left his grandchild's sporting event as soon as my call for help was received. My latch-key friend rushed to the hospital as quickly as possible to sit with me while waiting for any bit of information. Taken entirely by surprise, one of my friends unexpectedly showed up with a bag containing bottled water, fruit and snacks for me just so I could get through the day.

The following day, the caring husband of a good friend as well as his daughter came to lend support. My latch-key friend brought a friend who was a Deacon in her church. His kind words filled me with hope for my Prince's recovery. So many friends came for support, and those gestures meant the world to me.

Our favorite priest, the one who blessed the pups before we gave them up to advanced training, came to lend support to me as well as help my Prince on whatever journey God had in mind for him. His giving Prince Charming the Last Rites signaled the wrong ending of my fairy tale, but the right conclusion for my Prince if it came to that end. In any event, so many friends came to help me through the sadness of tragedy and extreme loss. Their actions demonstrated what the true concept of family meant...caring for someone in need.

    The Family of Friends as I called them didn't stop with the hospital stay. Following Prince Charming's passing, the support of friends continued with one friend showing up unexpectedly at the front door with a decorated lantern that contained a candle to light my way through the terrible journey I now faced. The thoughtful neighbors who shoveled my sidewalks and driveway each and every time it snowed were evidence of my having a wonderful Family of Friends.

The kind neighbor who brought over home-made soup and flowers to brighten my day helped in so many ways. My latch-key friend texted me on a daily basis just wanting to know if I needed anything; that concern meant everything to me. As the newly adopted member of their family, I was invited to lunches, Friday dinners and to their grandchild's theatrical events. There was also the sympathetic friend who frequently invited me to share breakfast with her and didn't care if I ended up crying over my loss. Nothing says friendship more than being able to cry over pancakes in public.

Then, there were the friends who seemed to know just when I was at my lowest ebb in terms of loneliness and would call to offer comfort and support while I cried from the sadness. Those phone calls helped me in ways that can never be repaid. All of my friends were taking care of me in many ways...I was truly lucky to have such a caring and kind Family of Friends.

Another type of family developed through membership in a Grief Support Group. While I was unlucky due to my loss of Prince Charming to qualify as a member, I was indeed fortunate to have found a degree of solace with those who experienced the sadness of loss in different manners. In the security of a confidential setting, hearing others share their experiences with loss opened my eyes to the enormous toll that menacing Grief took on each of us and still does in various ways. The group was the club that no one wanted to belong to, yet we all found ourselves being members and as such…a family.

The other family I considered close to my heart was the memory of our Puppy Family. Prince Charming and I shared almost fifteen years working with these puppies, and each puppy found a special place in our hearts. Our sunroom's Wall of Fame, containing pictures of the puppies, chronicled their lives while they stayed with us as well as their lives after leaving us for training to assist the disabled. We were just a small but loving chapter in their lives.

For the year spent in our household, each pup became a family member and was treated as such. Seeing their pictures with Prince Charming holding some of them reminded me of that Puppy Family bond that was shared for so many years and was now gone forever.

So, the concept of family varies from individual to individual. I am fortunate to have found a variety of families who were there when I needed help the most. That is exactly what families do for each other…

Never again will I concern myself with the absence of my birth family during the most difficult time of my life. I've learned that families come in all shapes and sizes. While I currently might not have had the traditional family to help with my grief, I do have the Family of Friends, the Grief Support Group as well as the Puppy Family who helped me through the most difficult time of my life and continue to do so on a daily basis.

I've learned that not everyone can live up to the expectations of family responsibilities…myself included…nor do they always have the courage to do so. My friends, members of the support group and the pups who trained with us managed to accomplish both the expectations as well as the courage. I am blessed in so many ways.

Crisis of Faith

Just for the record, I have always believed in God and trusted in His wisdom. However, in light of what recently happened, I am genuinely angry with Him and cannot accept the premise that He has a plan in terms of what happens to us in our daily lives. I simply refuse to be hypocritical and be certain of that belief. Perhaps God has a special agenda for each of us...but a simple plan? I don't think so.

Why would He have the need for so many souls in his heavenly entourage? He rules the earth so why the distinct need for troops? Prince Charming was the love of my life and the embodiment of goodness and kindness. Why did God need his soul with him in heaven when my Prince might have continued to do good works here on earth? Taking him so early just doesn't seem like a well-thought-out plan as far as I am concerned, and God should be the best planner in heaven and on earth. What was He thinking?

Prince Charming and I were religious in the sense that we attended weekly Mass and followed most of the church's doctrines. However, we did have our reservations with regard to some spiritual matters. We challenged some of the church's man-made philosophies and looked for spiritual guidance in various churches along the way.

For the most part, with the exception of our favorite priest and our two parish priests, we were pretty much disappointed in terms of the methods and messages given by individuals who allegedly represented the church's doctrines. We were looking for some relevant spiritual guidance for living our lives. That guidance was difficult to find with the church's reliance on pomp and circumstance rather than substance.

We were met with theatrics in the changes of the Mass as well as homilies that had no special significance to our daily lives. Still, we continued to attend the services in hopes of finding something of importance that might keep us coming back for more.

When discussing the changes in the church a few years ago, I was told by a church's representative that there were two groups of followers in the church: the sheep and the goats. The sheep, as required, blindly followed the church's rules without question and would eventually find their way through the heavenly gates. However, the ending was not so great for the goats who questioned some of the man-made rules as being doctrine. Instead, the goats relied upon good works and kindness to others. Their fates were not as clearly defined. But, my question was: Who gave mortal men the right as well as the audacity to pass judgement on others and define their fates? That judgement was left to God and to God alone.

That peculiar conversation years ago really stretched our beliefs and drove us further and further away from finding what was good and meaningful in our relationship with the church. As disappointed as we were, we continued our church attendance in hopes of one day finding something relevant.

Then, The Three Amigos struck, and even Prince Charming couldn't make it through the weekly service due to his trifecta of illnesses. I attended the services in his place hoping beyond hope that God would hear my pleas for help for my ailing Prince. Here was a good man who had done nothing but good for others, and he needed God's help. Nevertheless, no help came…not from God…nor from my numerous pleas to the saints as well as the hundreds of vigil lights lit for Prince Charming's health concerns. My beliefs in the power of prayer were totally shattered. Assistance in any form was nowhere in sight…from God or from his minions.

Speaking of minions…add insult to injury, after Prince Charming's untimely passing, that same church's representative never offered any form of support for me during the weeks and months that followed. Perhaps he had some reasons for being absent during my grief, but how does one represent and speak for the doctrines of the church and not live them in one's daily life? Not sure how that disparity fits in with a life of Christian charity, but for me, that hypocrisy sealed my crisis of faith.

God had suddenly taken my Prince and left nothing that might even come close to nurturing my soul. Due to my anger, I stopped going to church but found some form of consolation in the television version of the Mass on Sundays as well as relevance in the televised homilies.

On one occasion in an attempt to reconnect with my faith, I tried going back to the Sunday ritual. Because I didn't want to see the people who knew us as a team or for them to witness my grief, I sat in a different section of the church. Needless to say, nothing had changed except my feelings of being hypocritical at pretending to benefit from the service. If anything, I am not a hypocrite, so I left the service with tears in my eyes over yet another loss…the loss of hope that something might have changed.

A very dear friend of mine offered the possibility that perhaps God took my Prince to spare him further pain and suffering from his illnesses in the future. While I would like to consider that premise, my anger regarding the loss of Prince Charming is much too strong right now to allow even the smallest bit of acceptance of that idea. While it might sound reasonable in the future, it's not even close to acceptable in terms of my current reality.

Perhaps someday I'll find my way back to God, the church and alternate theories of loss. For now, as far as I am concerned, God didn't have a well-thought-out plan in terms of taking my Prince Charming's life and ultimately giving me no reasons for returning to the church. My crisis is ongoing.

I must admit that my anger toward God is not as intense as it was months ago, but those painful feelings are still there. Maybe in time, my anger will diminish altogether, and my faith will return. Anything is possible.

In the meantime, I carry Prince Charming's beloved wooden cross with me at all times with the hope of someday returning to my beliefs. In many ways, I hope that gesture helps. But, for now, my anger is still too strong in the midst of my unimaginable loss…

Never again will I feel the same way about religion as I did prior to the unbearable loss of Prince

Charming. My loss of faith has reached crisis proportions, and I am not sure how to ever get back to believing as I did. Maybe someday I will, but for now, my faith is shattered. Perhaps those goats who question the church's man-made rules but rely on their good works won't get the best seats in heaven after death. Who knows? While those goats might get rooms in heaven next to the ice machines, they will still make it through the pearly gates. Kindness and good works matter!

Life Goes On

Following the memorial service, I lived in what some might call a haze of disbelief. Unable to sleep at night due to the relentless crying as well as the fear of being alone in the house, I struggled during the day with attempts at brief naps. I would either curl up in Prince Charming's wicker chair or walk back and forth through the house...crying every step of the way. I didn't care that the mail piled up on the dining room table, dishes sat unwashed in the sink and televisions played endlessly in various rooms.

When I was not meandering through the house or peering out at the empty yard, I sat in Prince Charming's favorite recliner in the great room...the one he found so comforting following his chemotherapy sessions. I thought that if I tried hard enough, I might feel his arms around me offering comfort for the grief that had taken over my senses. But, no matter how hard I tried or how long I stayed in that recliner, no relief was ever in sight for me. The only consolation was a fleeting recollection of my Prince sitting there and resting comfortably. Even though that glimpse of him faded ever so quickly, I experienced a brief flash of closeness I hadn't felt in such a long time.

The days filled with tears were exhausting. I had to find some way to force myself into the world of the living if only to pay bills and organize what needed to be done. The stacks of mail were just getting higher and higher, and I needed to force myself into the machine-like mode again in order to get control of the sadness that filled my days and nights. I was totally lacking in motivation, but I still had countless responsibilities that necessitated my immediate attention.

Faced with the inner-workings of the household alone for the very first time, I found it necessary to revert to my standard practice of making lists based upon priorities. Numerous stacks of unopened mail, various magazines and outdated newspapers littered the surface of the dining room table. Nevertheless, I found great consolation in knowing that each stack had a purpose. Now, I just had to figure out what to do with each item as well as the best way to approach the situation.

For days, I sorted through stacks of mail. Some items were completely foreign to me in terms of what to do about them, but others were fairly easy to decipher. Government agencies were notified, bills were paid and sporting newspapers were cancelled. However, the challenge of all challenges remained at the far end of the table…the dreaded income tax information. I had a few weeks before the due date and only glanced at it once in a while during the day. That manila envelope, bulging at the seams with important papers, had been prepared throughout the year by my financially savvy Prince. While momentarily tempted to open the packet, I fought the urge and continued my procrastination of that challenge.

As the weeks progressed, I found myself switching automatically into my robotic mode in order to keep track of the bills and maneuver my way through my Prince's most intricate but exacting financial methods. His system was quite complicated due to his previous experience with banking. In the past, the closest I ever got to a successful financial system was making sure I put the check book in my purse when going shopping, and that gesture didn't come close to his financial wizardry. Needless to say, his structure was not working for me, so I found it necessary to devise my own in order to keep up with my current, financial situations. Prince Charming was the master of the check book, and I never approached his high level of competence.

One of the major decisions I had to make was selling Prince Charming's car. Insurance premiums were coming due, and I didn't need two cars. I really liked his car and was sad to make that decision to sell, but my car was more suited to my needs. Once again, my trusty latch-key friend accompanied me to the car dealership. I had already received an estimate of a selling-price from a neighbor, who worked for a car dealership, so I was confident I knew what to expect. The offer was right on target from my neighbor's estimate, so the sale was made. Seeing my Prince's car being driven away saddened me, but my current life was sad anyway so what did it matter? When I was in my robotic mode, there was no room for sentiment because it hurt too much. I'd have time for the tears once I got home. As soon as the garage door opened, I saw the empty space his car once occupied. Needless to say, tears flowed again…signifying another loss.

The next day while coming out of the grocery store, Grief was playing games with me again. As I headed towards my car, I couldn't believe what I saw and suddenly stopped in the middle of the crosswalk. The car parked next to mine was the exact color, make and model of Prince Charming's car.

That car couldn't possibly be my Prince's car. Was Grief now shifting from jerking me around to being cruel? Once I caught my breath and moved towards the parked car, I noticed a small dent in the bumper...proving it wasn't his. Even though I was filled with relief that the car next to mine wasn't Prince Charming's car, I just couldn't stop the tears from falling. Why won't this nightmare end?

Grief just couldn't resist jerking me around and in a matter of days found another way to bring me to tears. Prince Charming had ordered new license plates for his car months ago. I had forgotten that he had ordered the plates until they came in the mail...just days after I sold his car. But, receiving the new license plates wasn't the end of Grief's meddling. Prince Charming had ordered plates having not only our initials but also included the date of our wedding. Our fairy tale date was right there, front and back, etched on cheap metal. Even after death, my dear Prince continued to demonstrate his intense love for me.

    After recovering from the shock of receiving the special plates so soon after selling the car, I knew I had to make a dreaded trip to the Department of Motor Vehicles to get the new license plates assigned from Prince Charming's car to mine. Now, I knew of few people who actually left the Department of Motor Vehicles unscathed by the long lines, reprimands from clerks and, at times, some unusual situations. While fearful of this official visit, I was determined to handle any situation that arose. I wanted those special license plates on my car because they were another sign of Prince Charming's love for me.

Yes, there were long lines and impatient car owners crushing their vehicle titles in their hands while waiting for assistance. I just hoped for a nice representative who was having a relatively good day. What were the odds of that happening? The chances were not good since the gentleman in front of me was muttering words I hadn't heard in years, and his anger would probably infuriate the clerk. His actions accomplished that fact, and after concluding his business, he quickly left the facility...muttering strange words.

It was now my turn to face the situation as well as the fall-out from the previous customer. I calmly told the clerk of my recent change in marital situation, expressed my desire to have Prince Charming's plates re-assigned to my car and anxiously waited for her response. I was stunned as tears welled up in her eyes. She assured me that the plates ordered by my considerate Prince would be immediately re-assigned to my car. Seeing her tears, instantly brought tears to my eyes, and both of us were sniffling. The man in the next cubicle, stood up, saw us both teary-eyed and asked if he could help. I'll never know why that gentleman's actions seemed funny, but both the clerk and I started to laugh. After thanking him for his kindness and having the new license plates assigned to my car, I left the building with a smile on my face. That moment was truly significant because I'm sure that people rarely leave the Department of Motor Vehicles with a smile.

As I pulled into the driveway of our house, I knew I had to immediately change the license plates. I was going to ask my neighbor to help me, but my renewed spirit in the kindness shown toward others gave me the courage to do something without anyone's help. After investigating the position of the plates, I immediately knew what to do and changed those plates myself. Seeing our initials and our special date etched on the front and back plates of my car was bittersweet in that it was a reminder of not just the beginning of the fairy tale but the end as well.

The days, weeks and months seemed to fly by, and while at times I felt that I was getting better, something would occur that would set me back a few weeks in terms of dealing with my reality. During the week, I forced myself to get out of bed every morning, pay the bills and do the shopping. But, the dreaded weekends held those extra-special nightmares for me. Laundry was done, bills were paid and nothing awaited me as a distraction. The house that was once a place for love and laughter was now a quiet and lonely place.

My friends had their own lives and their own families. I certainly couldn't impose on them or their family time. I needed to find something to occupy my time during those dreaded hours and days of the weekends. Prince Charming and I did everything together for almost forty-five years. Finding something that held any degree of purpose was, indeed, a challenge.

In the past, working with a puppy in training was filled with adventures. We took the active puppy on numerous excursions to area county fairs, visited various restaurants or went people-watching at the nearby shopping mall.

Now, I either couldn't find anything that might fill the void on the weekends or just didn't have the energy to go out and do something alone. Grief has a way of sapping every bit of strength from one's body.

My weekends now consisted of endless hours of missing my Prince, intermitent bouts of intense crying or trying to figure out ways to move forward through this cycle of grief. One step forward just didn't seem to be enough to counteract the two steps backward that occured when even a bit of sunlight entered the picture. Grief had such a strong hold on my life…day and night…unrelenting in its severity. I wanted to feel better without short changing my total devotion to Prince Charming, but I couldn't find a way to accomplish that goal.

The Grief Support Group did wonders for my peace of mind, but I still needed some purpose for my life. My Prince and I had fifteen years of working with the dogs as well as my writing books about their experiences, yet I had nothing that was mine alone. Finding something as a purpose for the lonely weeks ahead was a goal of mine. Yet, nothing with regard to an idea was forthcoming.

Without my Prince, perhaps I had little to offer the world. Rather than face that possibility, I resorted to situating myself in my safe place in Prince Charming's favorite wicker chair for consolation. How did one face the future without one's soulmate? I was truly lost in terms of what to do.

Eight months passed, but tears and sadness were still my constant companions. Some days had glimmers of sunshine, and others held no reprieve from the sadness. Once again, I took one step forward and two steps backward. That was Grief's plan for me, and in time, I came to accept the inevitable. In spite of so many triggers related to the never-agains that Grief threw at me, I faced them, cried relentlessly but managed to recover each time. Thanks to Grief's enjoyment of my sadness, confronting those terrible triggers was the drill I faced on a daily basis.

I'd like to say that time has made my life quite a bit better in terms of dealing with my sadness, but to be honest, the weeks and months that passed haven't changed the daily experiences. That loop of events dealing with Prince Charming's treatments as well as those final days in the hospital when he lost his battle with The Three

Amigos circles my mind each night. There are also moments during the day that spell out his fight for life that can't ever be dismissed…just endured. As relentless as Grief's triggers may be, all I can do is deal with them as they occur. Thankfully, some days are quieter than others.

    Do I cry with the same intensity as I did when Prince Charming first passed away in my arms? I must admit that I don't, but I still cry every day when faced with the never-agains that chronicled our lives. Now, I just try to put them all in perspective in order to move forward with my life. I try to convince myself that I did the best I could for the man I loved with all my heart and all my soul. I just hope my efforts and decisions were enough to lessen his pain and suffering…

Never again would I work on our check books without feeling a responsibility to Prince Charming's legacy in terms of accuracy. While I won't devote hours to finding small sums as he did, coming as close as possible to exactness would fit my casual method of household accounting.

Never again would I see a car that looked like Prince Charming's and not feel a sense of loss and regret over selling it. Each time I look at my new license plates, I'm reminded of the wonderful life we had as well as the utter sadness for what was lost.

Never again will I feel his warmth and comfort in my life. Moving forward without him was expected of me, but how do I even begin that chapter in my life?

CONCLUSION

Holding the Winning Hand

For the last eight months, I had been on a quest to find ways to let go or lessen the powerful impact of the never-agains…those memories shared during our lives. Countless memories rumbled through my mind of my special life with Prince Charming, and after almost forty-five years of marriage, those never-agains popped up everywhere. I naively thought that letting go of them or decreasing the effect of Grief's triggers on the memories might help with the endless sorrow that filled my daily life. Sad to say, I was so very wrong in my attempts as well as my assessment of the powers of the never-agains.

Each day, I sought to find a way to deal with Grief's triggers that manifested themselves in the never-agains. Those devious triggers caused gut-wrenching emotions that would inevitably send me into some form of crying…either on the side of a road or to the comfort of Prince Charming's wicker chair…leaving only sadness in their wake.

I must admit, the pain of loss took over my life. When I first lost my Prince, I was convinced that I would die of a broken heart…that was how much my heart ached all day and all night. But, I had enormous responsibilities that were left to me by Prince Charming, and I had to fulfill those duties. Dying of a broken heart was not even a serious consideration until all responsibilities were fulfilled, and the house was cleaned.

Now, you might find at least one of my reasons for delaying dying of a broken heart to be frivolous, but what sort of person would leave cleaning the house, dealing with bills, selling cars and everything that was involved in home ownership to someone else? Those responsibilities were now mine and mine alone. My priorities were getting the house in order and dealing with the triggers haunting my never-agains.

In order for my original quest regarding the never-agains to be successful, I needed to move past impending obstacles. Those encounters originated in very close proximity in the form of Prince Charming's birthday quickly followed by our wedding anniversary. During those days, rather than resist the temptation to relive special moments, I sat in his favorite wicker chair and immersed myself in all of the wonderful events that happily occurred during the previous years. As painful as it was to remember all of those moments, I found the wide-ranging experience somewhat cathartic in spite of the tears of loss and sadness.

As the holidays approached, I dreaded Thanksgiving as well as the first Christmas in almost forty-five years without my Prince Charming. So many memories were associated with these special days. How does one get past the grief of being without the one person who was loved for so many years? I didn't have a clue.

Facing his birthday and our wedding anniversary was difficult, but the upcoming holidays were going to be extremely challenging since those never-agains were popping up at all times of the day and night. Was I even close to finding answers to my search for letting go of the never-agains? At best, would I even be able to lessen the painful impact of those memories? I needed answers in order to get through the holidays.

After months of soul-searching, I finally found answers to my quest. However, the answers came in the form of startling results. I concluded that there was actually no letting go of the never-agains nor was there any possibility of lessening the impact of Grief's triggers when they occurred. Those powerful and timeless memories in the form of never-agains, along with the terrible triggers, were permanent parts of my life with no possibility of ever letting go.

The key to the quest was not in the letting go of the never-agains, but in finding just the right corner of my mind for them as well as the special place in my heart for the feelings…for the rest of my life. While my original pursuit was a failure, the outcome was a complete success.

A few weeks after my startling conclusions about the never-agains, I was experiencing moments of extreme dread and wasn't sure why those feelings were occurring. I sensed a darkness in my body...like a part of me was missing. I know that sounds very strange, but the hollow feelings were so extreme that I could actually feel the emptiness within me. That sensation was completely unnerving.

At some point in time, I was overcome with a sense of clarity that explained all of my unfamiliar feelings. Prince Charming's passing took a huge chunk out of my life and created that void in me. The woman who was the Prince's soulmate was gone forever and would never return. I wasn't myself anymore and would have to find a way to move forward without him…as an entirely different person. Facing that startling realization was overwhelming, and I wasn't sure how to even begin to adjust to that person I had now become due to his loss. Was that type of adjustment even possible?

    A few days later in the midst of my confusion, I heard someone on television mention that looking at life through the rear-view mirror doesn't allow for looking forward to the possibilities of life in the future. I supposed that living in the past was exactly what I was doing. I was reliving those dreadful moments surrounding my Prince Charming's passing in the rear-view mirror of our special lives together…hoping for something that was never ever going to happen. The outcome was never going to change, and Prince Charming was never coming back to me.

In the midst of all that was going on in my life, I looked to any source of information for wisdom or comfort. I'd like to say that having a love of poetry caused me to dwell on the heartfelt words from one of the poems written by William Wordsworth, but that entire statement would not only be inaccurate but totally unrealistic.

I attributed my liking of his words from that particular poem to the television movie, *Splendor in the Grass* starring Natalie Wood and Warren Beatty. That movie was and always will be one of my favorite movies…not so much for the actors or the acting, but for William Wordsworth's touching words that reverberated throughout the movie's content and impact on the characters:

"Though nothing can bring back the hour
 Of Splendor in the grass,
 Of glory in the flower,
 We will grieve not, rather find
 Strength in what remains behind."

Those thought-provoking words might serve as a future guide for me in my quest for some sort of life without Prince Charming. Not only did I need to replace the negative never-agains in the rear-view mirror for the positive ones, but I also had to look ahead to a future life without him…as painful as that might be. Wordsworth's poignant words were both challenging and not easily followed while in the throes of grief. I was alone now with only the images in the rear-view mirror for my strength. Perhaps those images were all I needed to move forward and escape the emotional gridlock that filled my days.

Since I was now on my own and getting back to my reality, all of the usual household responsibilities were falling into place...the checkbooks were up to date or as close as I could maneuver, and the house was the cleanest it had ever been. There were days when my heart ached with such intensity for my loving Prince that I thought dying of a broken heart was surely a distinct possibility, and a great part of me welcomed the opportunity. However, those moments passed, and I eventually recovered from the brief episodes only to repeat the pain at some point in the days to come. Grief was having fun with me in such a cruel way.

In terms of the initial premise regarding letting go of my never-agains, my journey was not a successful venture, but I was glad of that fact. While some days were better than others, not a day went by that I didn't, at some point, recall memories shared throughout the years or relive those last moments of my Prince Charming's life. That recurring loop of his last moments revolved in my head and was etched in my brain forever. While reliving the memories was painful, letting go of them was not ever an option.

Remembering our blatant tossing of cholesterol levels to the wind while savoring fried shrimp on the wharf in San Francisco, hiking in the mountains of Lake Tahoe or relaxing under the California sun of Palm Desert were all never-agains that will give me, at some point, solace in the years to come.

The everyday never-agains like visualizing Prince Charming resting in his recliner, picturing his endearing smile, remembering his jokes, sharing special hugs, loving the sound of his laughter, holding hands wherever we went and so many more images were all safe and secure in those special places in my heart and mind.

If I had one wish, I'd wish for the last week of Prince Charming's life to be re-lived in a different way. The doctors would say that his issues were critical instead of treatable. I'd have moments to talk with my dear Prince about his concerns, discuss his last wishes and share loving thoughts about the years we spent together. Instead, I felt robbed of those opportunities due to his unpredictable and sudden passing. Those lost moments of sharing would haunt me for the rest of my life...he wasn't supposed to die!

To make life-changing decisions about a loved one was just so utterly distressing, yet that was exactly what happened when the unlikely tragedy occurred. While those critical decisions about his life were made with the best of intentions, I would live with their consequences for the rest of my life. If I could go back in time and relive the previous week, it would make all the difference in the world…not just for my peace of mind but also for the life of my Prince Charming.

    I know when most people make wishes for do-overs, they ask for an hour or just five minutes to spend with their loved one in order to make things right or say what they have to say. Call me an optimist, but I wanted my do-over with Prince Charming to last a week. After all, my request is just a wish that can't possibly come true. I might as well think big where the impossible is concerned!

Since my moments of dreaming for do-overs had passed, I was back to dwelling on my never-agains. There was just no letting go of them with regard to my life with Prince Charming. In spite of the pain, why would I ever want to let go and rob myself of the wonderful memories of his life so beautifully lived? What was I thinking of when I proposed this quest?

I wished that I had answers to the questions that continuously drifted around my mind regarding the reasons for Prince Charming's passing and my pursuit for insight. I'll never really have the answers to those questions but might find some workable way to make sense of my grief-stricken life…not without his memory, but with him smiling at me from the rear-view mirror of our lives together.

It seemed that now there were moments in my day that I held the winning hand in Grief's deck of cards. That winning hand might not seem like much to some, but to me, that successful hand was definitely a move in the right direction.

With any luck, some peace of mind will follow my winning hand over Grief's triggers in the years to come. I wish for and dream of that type of peace knowing my wishes and dreams are not entirely impossible…not compared to the impossibility of the do-over week I requested.

When my journey began, I had hoped that my quest for letting go of the never-agains would result in some level of closure for my unimaginable loss. Yet, I was completely wrong with regard to the results of my search. Instead of the closure I sought, finding a place for the never-agains in my heart and mind was not just the answer to my quest but the start of an entirely new journey....without Prince Charming. Hopefully, the fond recollections of the fairy tale life we shared for so many years together would guide me along that new path.

With those precious memories in the rear-view mirror of my life and guided by the touching words of William Wordsworth, perhaps I might gain strength and hope for a future without him. I also realized that even though our fairy tale ended, I still share that dream with him…now and for the rest of my life.

The treasured, wooden cross that meant so much to my Prince Charming now has a permanent place in my pocket, and carrying that cross means my Prince is with me where ever I go.

Our lives were so closely intertwined in our fairy tale…one that ended much too soon. While I originally wished for a do-over lasting a week, truth be told, I'd treasure even one last minute with my Prince.

By the way…my beloved Prince Charming's name is Chuck…

While our fairy tale ended abruptly without the happily ever after ending I envisioned, not everyone has the opportunity for a fairy tale in their lives. Prince Charming and I were fortunate enough to have had such a wonderful life together. Those cherished never-agains will be with me forever.

With great sadness in my heart, I find myself reluctantly saying…Farewell, my dear Prince…until we meet again.

The Author

Jennifer Rae Trojan, who sometimes writes as Jennifer Rae, lives in a suburb of Chicago, Illinois. Since retirement as a high school guidance counselor, Jennifer has worked with various assistance dog organizations serving as a puppy raiser, a puppy sitter and volunteer with animal assisted therapy. In addition to these activities, Jennifer gives presentations at libraries, in schools and to community groups regarding the role of the assistance dog and how it relates to the writing of her books about the dogs.

Letting Go of the Never-Agains, A Journey of Love and Loss, is very different from her other books and is a tribute to her dear husband Chuck who passed away on January 23, 2018. Her journey of loss is a true labor of love with regard to their relationship as well as a farewell to their fairy tale that ended much too soon.

Acknowledgements

Writing this book has taken me through the intense journey of the personal loss of a loved one…my dear husband Chuck. He was taken from my life much too soon but left a legacy of good works and kindness to all who knew him. I'd sincerely like to thank first and foremost:

Chuck Trojan, the love of my life and best friend ever, shared our fairy tale romance for almost forty-five years. When people asked how we managed to stay together for so many years, he would jokingly say that he had lost a bet. However, I won that bet, and my life with him was the grand prize!

Frances Splitgerber, my latch-key friend, shadowed me through the most horrible moments and days of my life and still lends support on a daily basis. Our lasting friendship began in elementary school and continues to this day…even to the point of including me in her family's luncheons, dinners and events. She has made me feel like a member of her family…something I needed so much at this terrible time in my life.

Kim Stephenson of PawPrints Pix Photography for her expertise in the cover designs. Her talents are limitless, and her patience with my endeavors is much appreciated.

Pam Osbourne for her talents in formatting, proofreading and assistance with the publishing of this book. First and foremost, she is my friend and thanking her just doesn't seem like enough praise for someone who has helped me so much over the years.

Kathleen Deist for her expertise in terms of proofreading skills as well as her acting as a consultant in the formation of this book. She is also a dear and most comforting friend who has been at my side through the most difficult time of my life.

Carol DeMaio whose expertise in terms of proofreading and constructive criticisms provided numerous insights into some of the changes in the book …not to mention her dear and lasting friendship that helped me through so many difficult days since my husband's passing. She always seems to know just the right time to give me a phone call.

Father Slawek Ignasik for his words of comfort for me as well as for Prince Charming during the most trying times of our lives. His words strengthened me for a life without my husband as well as prepared my husband for a life with God. How does one thank a person for that?

The Family of Friends touched my heart through their visits, their calls at a time when comfort was most needed as well as the numerous ways they helped me through my devastating loss. I can never repay the kindness but will always remember the goodness shared from friends.

Christine McMinn, LCPC, of the Living Well Cancer Resource Center who not only facilitated the Grief Support Group but also gave me insights and challenges into my dealings with loss and grief. I will always be grateful for her assistance as well as her ability to see through my bravado and offer some challenging possibilities for my dealing with loss in a healthy and productive way.

The Grief Support Group from the Living Well Cancer Resource Center whose weekly sharing of personal loss and experiences assisted in helpful ways too numerous to mention. Their sharing of emotional aspects of their lives as care givers helped me on my road from the extreme loss of my beloved husband. I am so very grateful for their support and assistance.

The Puppy Family who graced our lives for fifteen years and brought laughter and love to our household. Training each puppy was a true labor of love. While their spending a year with us was just a brief chapter in each of their lives, that special year is etched in our hearts forever.

P.S.

If I might impart a few words of advice learned the hard way: Share your final wishes with your loved ones. Give them the peace of mind knowing they are fulfilling your wishes. Making life decisions without your guidance leads to regrets that cloud the mind and last forever.

I sincerely thank you for sharing my past and present journey with love and loss.

Jennifer Rae Trojan